"It was a deeply satisfying experience professionally and personally to work with Diamond Rio."

— MARTIN SHEEN,
Actor

"Diamond Rio is a great group who I've been personal friends with for 10 years. I have a tremendous amount of respect for what they do on the stage, and just as importantly, for what they do offstage. Giving back is something we have in common. We're both very passionate about helping others, and Diamond Rio's work with Big Brothers and Big Sisters of Middle Tennessee is very impressive. They've made a difference in a lot of kids' lives and encouraged others to do the same. They're great friends and I'm proud to know them."

— TONY STEWART,
Champion NASCAR driver, owner,
philanthropist

"I've been friends with Diamond Rio for almost fifteen years. The guys in the group have been there for me in tough times and blessed moments—including Brian and Dana standing up with me at my wedding, Marty singing "The Lord's Prayer," and all of the guys playing their special music for the reception! The reason I tell you that is because the beauty of *Beautiful Mess* is that you will get to know the guys in the band as I do—six terrific, talented musicians who are also dedicated, loyal friends. This book pulls no punches; you'll read about both the good times and bad. But, most of all—just like Diamond Rio—you'll discover *Beautiful Mess* to be both entertaining and inspiring. And, that's something we need lots more of in the world today.

— SCOTT McKAIN,
Best-selling author / professional
speaker

"I had the honor of writing some songs with the Diamond Rio guys. During our time together, I was given an inside look at the story and faith of this legendary group, and it was clear to me why their music continues to touch so many lives."

— MATTHEW WEST,
Contemporary Christian recording
artist and writer

"Diamond Rio is not only a stellar group of artists who have entertained multitudes for years, more importantly they are the real deal when it comes to giving back to the community. The guys have been wonderful ambassadors for Big Brothers Big Sisters for more than a decade. The love and support they have given so selflessly to help uplift some of the most vulnerable of our children in this country is truly remarkable. What is most impressive is that they are truly nice guys who do it because they feel called to do so, and not for headlines. This book gets beneath the surface and reveals why these nice guys finish first!"

— LOWELL PERRY, JR.,
CEO, Big Brothers Big Sisters of
Middle Tennessee

"What an inspiring picture! Finding the reality of God's plan for us in the midst of the messes we deal with in this life truly is beautiful. These guys continue to be heroes of mine on so many levels . . ."

— MIKE WEAVER
of "Big Daddy Weave"

BEAUTIFUL MESS

by

Diamond Rio

with
Tom Roland

THOMAS NELSON
Since 1798

NASHVILLE   DALLAS   MEXICO CITY   RIO DE JANEIRO   BEIJING

Published in Nashville, Tennessee, by Thomas Nelson. Thomas Nelson is a registered trademark of Thomas Nelson, Inc.

Published in association with the literary agency of Esther Fedorkevich, Fedd and Company Inc., 9759 Concord Pass, Brentwood, TN 37027.

Thomas Nelson, Inc., titles may be purchased in bulk for educational, business, fund-raising, or sales promotional use. For information, please e-mail SpecialMarkets@ThomasNelson.com.

Library of Congress Cataloging-in-Publication Data:

Diamond Rio (Musical group)
 A beautiful mess / by Diamond Rio with Tom Roland.
  p. cm.
  ISBN 1-59555-268-5
  1. Diamond Rio (Musical group) 2. Country musicians—United States—Biography.
I. Roland, Tom. II. Title.
ML421.D53D53 2009
782.421642092'2—dc22
 [B]   2009025250

Printed in the United States of America

09 10 11 12 13 QW 6 5 4 3 2 1

DEDICATION

We would like to dedicate this book to all the people out there who are struggling through some situation with seemingly no way out. We hope in some way that our story will encourage you to realize that God has not forgotten you and He has a purpose for you. Whatever it is, He can see you through it. Our prayer is that your "mess" may become "beautiful."

"What a beautiful mess I'm in."

—DIAMOND RIO

TABLE OF CONTENTS

EDGE OF DISASTER

July 4, 2005, Riverfront Park, Nashville, Tennessee

For years Diamond Rio managed to keep its internal issues a little-known secret.

As members of the legendary Grand Ole Opry and strong examples of musical craftsmanship, the band's six musicians had made a collective mark as a conglomeration of exacting players and sturdy personalities.

Now, on a 2005 Fourth of July stage, the secret was literally out in the open, broadcast to a national TV audience. The band that owned a reputation as a fine-tuned hit-making machine was sputtering, and it took just three songs to send the message.

Emcee Storme Warren introduced Diamond Rio to tens of thousands of fans along the Cumberland River that day as an act with a reputation for being "meticulous." But the sound that emanated from the television speakers at home and at Nashville's Riverfront Park—during GAC's (Great American Country) *Music City Independence Day Concert Spectacular*—failed to match the description. It was neither meticulous nor spectacular.

Lead singer Marty Roe clawed at the notes during the verses, arching his eyebrows with each phrase in the music, an attempt to seemingly will every passage into pitch. He missed the mark, however, more often than he hit it. It was uncomfortable to hear, practically an advertisement to the viewers at home to turn to another station.

As a listener, it was easy to write off the poor performance to sound problems—especially after the first song, "Beautiful Mess." As Marty introduced the next number, bass player Dana Williams motioned frantically to someone offstage to make adjustments in his monitor. Perhaps the guys just weren't hearing themselves properly.

But changing audio settings didn't help. As the group plowed through the rest of the set, the sound continued to deteriorate, particularly during the choruses when Diamond Rio's scintillating harmonies should have been at their most distinguished. Instead of the edgy, classy blend that had become their signature, the vocals were an amateurish collision. Marty and Dana were wishy-washy at best, and mandolin player Gene Johnson—whose tenor gave the harmonies their high-lonesome, quasi-bluegrass texture—seemed lost and out of place in the stratosphere.

The band members forged on bravely, keeping their emotions in check and playing to the cameras as if nothing was wrong. But it was difficult. It was the first time they'd played a date in Nashville in years. This was an all-American gig in front of their neighbors, and they were blowing it. They had friends and family who'd come out just to see them, the crowd was dotted with fellow musicians and entertainment-business insiders, and they weren't cutting it.

© Nashville Convention & Visitor Bureau

Left to Right: Jimmy Olander, Gene Johnson, Marty Roe, Dana Williams. July 4, 2005, Riverfront Park, Nashville, Tennessee.

"Trying to cowboy up during those three songs and make eye contact with people you know and love, it's one of the most uncomfortable situations you'll ever be in," guitarist Jimmy Olander says.

The show couldn't end fast enough. It was bad. Most of them knew it. They hoped their reputation as pristine players and perfectionists would give them some leeway with the public. People hear what they want to hear, and they loved this band—six nice guys with heartland roots and a classic work ethic.

Diamond Rio had launched twenty-five singles into the Top 20 on the *Billboard* country charts. The group had inspired fans with its joyous 1991 debut, "Meet in the Middle." It had induced reflection with the 2001 ballad "One More Day," adopted by many as a theme for personal commitment and later as a post–9/11 memorial to departed friends and family. The guys had cemented a place as sonic technicians with the intricate and inventive harmonies on 2002's "Beautiful Mess."

Playing a subpar concert in Music City was a tough pill to swallow. Some fans in the Fourth of July audience might overlook the pitch issues, but the band knew the professional musicians who were there could not. The Nashville Symphony had backed Diamond Rio during the concert, and now some of the town's most astute players—many of whom probably knew the band's name but perhaps not much of its work—likely suspected the group was a fake. And the pros in the country-music business, the people who knew the band's history well, had now been alerted to the secret.

Drummer Brian Prout stuck around after the performance to listen to Jamie O'Neal and Charlie Daniels and to watch the Independence Day fireworks. The crackling light display and the holiday's patriotism lifted his spirits, but a familiar face put a miserable coda on the experience.

Tim DuBois spotted Brian milling through the crowd at the end of the night and called out his name. Fifteen years earlier, Tim had been the head of Arista Records. He had signed Diamond Rio to its first record deal in 1990, had coproduced the group's first six years of hits, and had given the guys an unusual degree of latitude. While most mainstream country bands are forced to sit on the sidelines while studio musicians play the instrumental parts on their sessions, Tim's belief in Diamond Rio's abilities had given them a unique position on Music Row. They were one of the few commercially successful bands that played exclusively on its own recordings, and that was historically one of the strengths of Diamond Rio's live shows. The sound they got in the studio should have been replicated fairly well during the concert that day—but it was not. Tim knew something was wrong.

"Did you guys have trouble hearing on stage today or what?" he asked.

"Well, no," Brian replied. "Actually, the sound was pretty decent."

"Well, Marty didn't hear worth a darn," Tim said flatly.

Brian made a few excuses: Marty hadn't been feeling well. The temperature at sound check had been around one hundred degrees, and maybe the humidity had affected the sound system's responsiveness by the time the concert got under way.

Brian didn't think Tim was buying the story, and frankly he'd grown weary of covering up. It wasn't the first time Marty had sounded bad. In fact, he'd been singing poorly for at least three and a half years. As the drummer, Brian was the only band member who didn't play a melodic instrument, and he'd mostly left it to the other guys to talk with their front man about the poor-quality performances they were delivering.

Brian didn't make any confessions to DuBois that Fourth of July, but the chance encounter "was the straw that broke the camel's back," Brian confesses. "Quite honestly, I postured myself as, *Who am I to tell Marty Roe he can't sing?* That'd be like him comin' to me and saying I don't know how to play drums. So I kind of went up there and did my job and left him to Gene and Dana and maybe even to a large degree Jimmy and [keyboard player] Dan [Truman], who had a better understanding of the structure of melody and tone and notes than I do."

But after years of mostly sitting back and staying out of it, Brian took the muzzle off. He relayed Tim's derisive evaluation of Marty's performance to the other four, all of whom agreed with the assessment. They convened a group meeting during a trip to California and confronted their lead singer. It wasn't the first time they'd done it, but they had to try again.

"Marty, you can't sing anymore."

"It wasn't all that bad," he insisted. "I watched it on TV."

The band was incredulous, Brian recalls. "Jimmy or Dana said, 'Marty, if you're hearin' that and thinkin' it's not all that bad, then you're havin' some serious hearing problems. *It wasn't all that bad?* Dude, it was awful!'"

The battle lines had been drawn. One of country music's most successful and unified bands was no longer in harmony, on stage or off.

Diamond Rio's sole lead singer, Marty Roe, was the focal point of the group's public identity. He did more than half the interviews, he told the jokes and stories on stage, and he was the first human voice on most of their songs. To a man, the other guys loved Marty. He was the front man for the group, and his voice—more than any other element in the band— was the most identifiable sound for its fans. The slight Southern accent— acquired in his hometown of Lebanon, Ohio, a thirty-minute drive from the Kentucky border—lent a working-class authenticity to his unusually gifted abilities.

© NCVB

Marty–July 4, 2005

He possessed an uncanny range in tone and in volume that allowed him to wring the emotions from a song and still maintain a decidedly masculine sound. He could sing a spiritually direct song such as "I Believe" with conviction. He could portray the personal trauma of an alcoholic's self-inflicted pain in "You're Gone" as if it were his own. He could get downright goofy in "How Your Love Makes Me Feel" and still maintain his dignity.

But he wasn't making the grade. Everyone else in the group knew it, everyone *around* the group knew it, and it was just a matter of time before the rest of the Nashville music industry would know it as well. Marty had already taken steps to correct the problem and had made some improvements, which only goes to show how far things had fallen. The Fourth of July show had been mangled, and it was an improvement!

A DESPERATE LOYALTY

Marty had seen two vocal coaches. The band had reworked the material so that Dana sang many of Marty's parts during the harmony sections, a move Marty found personally humiliating. Diamond Rio even employed two tuners on stage to fix his vocal errors and dropped his voice so low in the mix that many in the audience had trouble hearing him at all.

The band and its crew had taken every step possible to hide the problem, but it was now in the open. Few people outside the group had confronted Marty about it. But after the GAC special, his partners began to hear the questions from their friends and families: "You guys are too good for that." "Are you gonna let him ruin your career?" "Are you gonna let the ship go down?"

"We had many heart-to-hearts there on the bus, the six of us just sittin' there tryin' to figure it out, Marty with his head bowed," Dana says. "I remember sittin' there one time sayin', 'Hey, man, here's the bottom line: We all started this together, and I intend on endin' this together. If that means this is the way it ends, then that means this is the way it ends. But I'm here to stand beside you, Marty, because the simple fact of the matter is we have stood beside one another, sung beside one another, through some of the greatest moments of my life.' We were havin' a real serious issue; I'll be dogged if I'm gonna bail out then. And you know what? I was there, and I would smile and grin and make every excuse I could make, as long as he was tryin' to make it better."

Marty had been trying, but whatever improvement he experienced was marginal, and he had run out of ideas. The band continued to work the road steadily during the next year, playing its shell games with the sound, hoping they could dodge the issue until some *ah-ha* moment of inspiration led to a cure.

Finally, during the summer of 2006, Jimmy called Marty in yet another attempt to find a solution. Marty's reaction startled the guitarist.

"He's tellin' me, 'Man, the more you're tellin' me about this, the more freaked out I get,'" Jimmy recalls. "This was a very emotional conversation, and we don't have big, emotional conversations. We're roommates on the road, but I'm not a super touchy-feely kinda guy, and neither is he."

Marty said he would do anything Jimmy asked in order to try and regain control of his vocal talent. And then the tears began to flow. "I don't know that I'm ever gonna get this back," he cried. "I feel like I've squandered it, and it's very possible that I've had my chance."

As long as Marty was willing to keep trying, Jimmy was confident the band would follow him to the end. He could only see two possible conclusions: either Marty would improve, or Diamond Rio was done.

chapter 2

TENNESSEE RIVER BOYS

© 2009 Grand Ole Opry Archives

*D*iamond Rio's professional life in 2005 was a tumultuous roller coaster, appropriate since the band could trace its beginnings to an amusement park. Opryland opened in Nashville in May 1972 with the usual theme park array of thrill rides, midway games, souvenirs, and cotton candy.

The tourist attraction's parent company, the National Life and Accident Insurance Company, also owned the Grand Ole Opry and made a point of emphasizing that musical connection in branding the venture. The Opry radio show first aired on WSM-AM in November 1925. Its rural-themed variety format soon established the Opry as the leader among what were then known as "barn dance" programs. The WSM signal covered much of eastern America, and the Saturday Opry shows went national when NBC's radio network added the program in 1939. Because of its association with that radio program, Opryland was built with a heavier emphasis on music than most theme parks.

The Grand Ole Opry House opened on the park's grounds in March 1974, providing a modern, suburban home for the Opry after thirty-one years at the downtown Ryman Auditorium. *The Porter Wagoner Show* and *Hee Haw* began taping their syndicated episodes in the Opryland production studios, in the same building as the Opry House. The park's Roy Acuff Theater took its name from a country legend. And one of Opryland's most popular rides, the Wabash Cannonball, drew its name from one of Roy's best-known hits. Roy, in fact, moved to a home on the Opryland property in 1983, the same year that the park's new ownership, the Gaylord Entertainment Company, inaugurated The Nashville Network (TNN)—a cable station that put a country stamp on such established TV formats as talk shows, variety programs, and talent contests.

During tourist season Opryland scheduled a heavy stream of live performances that aimed to attract every potential age group. *I Hear America Singing* examined folk and traditional pop from various regions across the country; *Rocking Around the Clock* was a standard '50s revue; and *Country Music USA* told the history of Nashville's best-known musical genre with a cast of singers imitating the likes of Hank Williams, Jim Reeves, and Patsy Cline.

Its Music City location guaranteed the park could tap into a rich vein of talent, and numerous songwriters and musicians hooked up with

Opryland jobs while trying to immerse themselves in the Middle Tennessee music community.

TENNESSEE RIVER BOYS: CONNECTING THE PLAYERS

It was in that atmosphere that a couple of park employees—Matt Davenport and Danny Gregg—put together a group for a one-time TV performance in 1982 that would promote Opryland on a local station. They billed themselves as the Grizzly River Boys, calling attention to a new log flume–style ride, the Grizzly River Rampage, and they impressed both the television station and their bosses at the park. The first appearance turned into a second, and Opryland soon gave them their own show built around a trio of singers—Matt, Danny, and Ty Herndon—who swapped lead voices, told jokes, and balanced old-school country concert shtick with a contemporary sound.

None of the players who would eventually make their mark in Diamond Rio were affiliated with the Grizzly River Boys at its start. And no one knew what a significant breeding ground of talent the group would become. In addition, no one was particularly fond of the name. In short order the Grizzly River Boys became the Tennessee River Boys, paying a nod to the park's setting along the Cumberland. Even the new name wasn't quite appropriate. Bluegrass pioneers such as Bill Monroe and Ralph Stanley had identified their bands with geographic imagery— the Blue Grass Boys and the Clinch Mountain Boys—so the Tennessee River Boys' moniker often led park visitors to expect an old-timey or rustic sound instead of the rock- and pop-influenced brand of country the group represented.

The name Tennessee River Boys had, in fact, been used in the past by two different acts. A bluegrass duo recorded for Mercury during the early 1950s under the banner Paul & Roy & the Tennessee River Boys, and an

R & B group, Rambling Rufus Shoffner & His Tennessee River Boys, cut some tracks that same decade.

Despite the anachronistic name, the Tennessee River Boys quickly developed a following—not just among Opryland season-ticket holders, but also among some of the musicians who played with established stars at the Opry. That included Dana Williams, a bass player who worked with Jimmy C. Newman. His high school music teacher, Al DeLeonibus, played piano for the River Boys, and whenever Jimmy C did an Opry matinee, Dana would take in at least one of the River Boys' performances at the Gaslight Theater.

"I'd go over and see the Tennessee River Boys play during the day, and I'd see my buddy Al DeLeonibus playin' with them," Dana recalls. "Then I'd come back and do an Opry spot and go back and listen there. They played two hundred sets a day or somethin'."

The Oak Ridge Boys were one of only a handful of groups having success in country music at the time, and all four Oaks got opportunities to sing lead at their shows. The River Boys took the same approach.

"Danny Gregg, he was a showman and a half," Dan Truman notes. "He was so good off the top of his head. He was funny and had so much good energy. Matt was just a rock. He could sing lead and harmonies, and he was a great musician."

Notwithstanding their group approach to the vocals, Ty Herndon was the main attraction, and it didn't take long for the Opry bosses to recognize it. When Ed McMahon started the syndicated TV competition *Star Search* in 1983, Opryland suggested Ty as a first-year contestant and he went all the way to the finals, bested only by Oklahoma-bred pop singer Sam Harris. Ty won a significant payoff in the process and decided it was time to pursue life as a solo performer. It took him nearly a decade, but he eventually grabbed the brass ring with a series of country hits, beginning with "What Mattered Most" in 1995.

In the meantime Al DeLeonibus told Dana the Tennessee River Boys were looking for a replacement: "Yeah, Ty finally quit, man. The chicks are goin' nuts over this guy."

That set up a short-lived revolving door in the River Boys' third vocal spot. Anthony Crawford—who would go on to work as a backup vocalist on albums by Rosanne Cash, Dwight Yoakam, and Steve Winwood—took over Ty's position for a while. He left for a tour with Neil Young and was replaced by another park employee, Virgil True, for much of the '84 season.

Marty Roe

Virgil likewise got a job with a touring act, and Danny Gregg and Matt Davenport turned to Marty Roe, who was doing Larry Gatlin imitations in Opryland's *Country Music USA* show, to finish out the year. The band had become acquainted with him when Marty performed on a TNN show Danny had hosted, and they knew his back-of-the-throat twang would provide a diversion from the pop-inflected vocals they were already offering as they passed the lead slot around from song to song.

"It was a good-payin' gig—paid better than what I was makin'," Marty recalls. "They had some road dates they wanted me to do, and they were talkin'—Alabama had hit in 1980, and this was '84—and they had this idea to go and do something like that, get a record deal. We *were* in Nashville."

Dan Truman

At the close of the '84 season, Gaylord head honcho Ed Gaylord brought a group of Opryland performers to the Oklahoma State Fair to showcase his company in his hometown with a ten- or twelve-day run. *Country Music USA* rotated two casts at the park—a red cast and a blue cast—with the former unofficially considered the lead crew. Performers from the red cast formed the backbone of the band at the Oklahoma fair, and Opryland officials recruited musicians from other park shows to fill out the roster. Marty, who still remembered much of the *Country Music USA* script and music, was a natural addition, as was Dan Truman, the piano player from *Country Music USA*'s blue cast.

Dan had been extremely active just months before, one of three keyboardists who worked a TNN show at $220 a pop in addition to his regular role in the park's productions. But the TV show had been canceled, Opryland's seasonal live shows were closing for the winter, and his $1,000-a-week paychecks had suddenly dried up. Dan earned a paltry $265 for the entire month of November. So the Oklahoma gig was quite welcome.

"It was cool," Dan says. "I had ten more days of work, and I said I'd do it. Well, Marty was one of the singers in that show. They used their best singers to showcase Opryland in Oklahoma City, and that's where we got to know each other."

After years of playing the road with show bands and pushing himself to practice daily, Dan easily impressed Marty with his skills. Little did Dan know he was laying the groundwork for his next job.

Before the 1985 season began at Opryland, Al DeLeonibus—convinced that Ty's departure meant the Tennessee River Boys had no commercial future—quit the band. Their drummer, Ed Mummert, dropped out as well. Marty suggested Dan and the Oklahoma-fair drummer, Jimmy "J. J." Whiteside, and the River Boys were again completely staffed. For a week or two anyway.

Larry Beard, the group's guitar player, had hoped to join the vocal ranks in the band. When Marty filled Ty's slot, Larry felt he had hit the proverbial glass ceiling and decided to move along. He clearly had some abilities—he would later play on albums by the likes of BlackHawk, Craig Morgan, and Billy Joe Royal—and his departure left a major gap in the Tennessee River Boys. In need of a replacement, the River Boys held an audition in March 1985 at the Musicians Union on Music Row, across the alley from the Sound Stage, a recording studio that had recently hosted sessions that yielded hits for George Strait, Conway Twitty, and the Statler Brothers.

Jimmy Olander

In that professional setting the band hoped it could land the kind of guitarist who would help build the commercial flair they were after. Or, at the very least, pick up the slack after Larry's departure.

Jimmy Olander had worked at Opryland before, so he knew the drill. He had done his time in *Country Music USA,* then left to go on the road with a bar band. He graduated to become a sideman for Mel McDaniel, who was getting regular airplay at the time with "Louisiana Saturday Night," "Big Ole Brew," and the aptly titled "I Wish I Was in Nashville."

Jimmy had quit Mel's band to try and stay closer to home in Music City. He had a wife to support and an idea that he could break into the ranks of Nashville's session guitarists. He was playing somewhat steadily on Nashville's fabled Printers Alley. But good musicians are plentiful in Music City, so the paycheck at those clubs was dismal. The studio work hadn't come as quickly as he had anticipated, and he needed a job. Jimmy wasn't particularly enthralled with the prospect of returning to Opryland. But *that* gig beat *no* gig. He could bear it for one season.

"I was gonna be there six months—that's it," Jimmy says. "I gave 'em a false promise: 'Oh yeah, I'm a candidate. I need a job.' I'd already been on the road in a tour bus, and these guys were in a band pulling a trailer and they didn't have much work. They were from Opryland, and oh, I judged this [as], *This is way, way below me.*"

Jimmy's disdain was not out of the ordinary among those with aspirations in the commercial recording business. Music Row's bread and butter came from creating new material and building stars. Shows like

Country Music USA were centered on covering the hits and mimicking established stars.

"That's not the real world," Jimmy explains. "That's not goin' out and findin' gigs and makin' a livin'. You actually do punch a time clock, and you go put your uniform on and perform a show, and there's a script of bits that have been written for you. It's not the real world. That's not music!"

©1983–84 Brian Rawlings

Left to right: Jimmy Olander, Marty Roe, Mel Deal, Matt Davenport, Danny Gregg, J. J. Whiteside, Dan Truman. "Jimmy had a beard when he auditioned and had to shave it because Opryland didn't allow beards." —Marty

Jimmy made a point during the audition to not share his hostile philosophy about Opryland with his prospective bandmates, who were instantly intrigued by his sound. Jimmy played a newly developed guitar, a Telecaster with a double-bender, an attachment that allowed him to raise the tone of one or two notes at a time. The guitar was barely heard of among professionals, let alone in amusement-park bands.

"I didn't even know what he was doin' at the time," Marty says, laughing. "It was the wildest thing, a really different sound. And it was really good."

Which made the Tennessee River Boys' decision fairly easy.

"Three guys showed up; Jimmy was the best," Dan says. "It's that simple."

The River Boys and their readjusted lineup—Danny Gregg, Marty Roe, and bass-playing Matt Davenport on vocals; Dan Truman playing piano; Jimmy Olander on guitar; Mel Deal on steel guitar; and J. J. Whiteside pounding the drums—tried to make some inroads at record labels that summer. They soon discovered that Jimmy's contempt for Opryland was fairly commonplace on Music Row.

OPRYLAND: HELP OR HINDRANCE?

The park had launched some talents to be sure—former Opryland employee Deborah Allen got a Grammy nomination for her heartbreaking 1984 hit "Baby I Lied"; *Country Music USA* alum Dean Rutherford, working under the professional name Dean Dillon, had already written George Jones's "Tennessee Whiskey," Hank Williams Jr.'s "Leave Them Boys Alone," and George Strait's "Unwound"; and bass player Don Cook had penned John Conlee's "Lady Lay Down" and the Oak Ridge Boys' "Cryin' Again." But the park still had that second-rate reputation that was tough to overcome.

"When you were at Opryland, there was a stigma about you," Jimmy says. "Cheesy, showbiz, *Up with America*—whatever that was—it was that thing. It's probably why when I joined the band, I had that [attitude] as well."

In his planned six-month tenure, however, Jimmy saw a side of the Boys he hadn't expected. There was talent in the band, along with a drive to become something bigger, not just a copy band that counted on an Opryland paycheck. They attracted the attention of Len "Snuffy" Miller—who'd played drums for Bill Anderson and produced the 1975 Kenny Starr hit "The Blind Man in the Bleachers"—and he took them in the studio, crossing his fingers he could get them a deal on Music Row.

They recorded three songs, with Matt, Danny, and Marty each taking the lead vocal on one.

"Variety is what kept us our gig out at Opryland, 'cause you're playing [for ages] two to ninety-two," Marty says. "We felt like that was a strength, that we could play all kinds of different styles, so we recorded that way."

Snuffy shopped them around to Nashville's labels during 1985 but found no takers. Warner Bros. chief Jim Ed Norman, however, must have heard something he liked. He took the time to counsel the group.

"[Jim Ed] asked, 'What are you guys? Are you a country band?'" Marty recalls. "'Well, we can do whatever you want.' That was our attitude. Jim Ed said, 'No, you gotta make a decision [about] who you are, what you wanna be. Pick one.' That was good advice. We didn't really wanna hear it at the time, but it was good advice, so I credit him for helpin' us to understand that these record labels, they ain't gonna figure it out for you. You gotta figure it out yourself."

BREAKING LOOSE: ON THE ROAD

One thing the Tennessee River Boys figured out for sure: they needed to leave Opryland at the end of the 1985 season.

"We felt Opryland was great," Marty says. "We were able to make a living playing music, we were in Music City U.S.A., we were close to the action and [thought] we should be able to get discovered. Music Row completely discredited what we did out there because it was a bunch of kids and 'They're not real musicians. They're not real artists.' So we quit. We quit the park."

"Nobody would take it seriously," Dan adds. "We'd kinda had that counseled to us: get out of there, and get in the real world. And then it took six years."

The band's manager, Steve Thurman, worked at the Top Billing booking agency, which procured concerts for the likes of Ronnie McDowell, Mel McDaniel, and comedian Jerry Clower, who "Snuffy" Miller produced. Tandy Rice, who owned Top Billing, got the River Boys work on the road when he could, but they didn't have hits or much of a name outside the Opryland grounds. At least they had equipment. Letting the other artists use it made them a little more attractive to the headliner and to concert promoters, who were always looking for ways to cut costs.

"We were making investments in sound systems so that we could get a gig," Marty says. "So that was really a big reason why we were [working much at all]—the fact that they had an opening act with a sound system. That's how they looked at it. We looked at it that, oh, we've got a gig."

The River Boys also supplemented their calendar by signing up with New York's Columbia Artists Management to do subscription dates. The agency acted as a clearinghouse for community concert series in smaller towns that had little access to top-level entertainment. Residents bought season tickets that entitled them to attend a range of performances by different acts, similar to the subscriptions that fine-arts organizations sell to their members in larger cities.

Productions such as the Guy Lombardo Big Band, the Blind Boys of Alabama, or *Irving Berlin Century*—featuring traditional pop songs written by one of America's best-known composers—exposed subscribers to swing music, gospel, and show tunes. The Tennessee River Boys added a youthful component to the series and contributed country to the stylistic blend.

There was nothing glamorous about the locations. They played high school auditoriums or small outdoor parks in places like Waukegan, Illinois; Wellsboro, Pennsylvania; and Reidsville, North Carolina. Their tour schedules were concentrated—four or six weeks long at the most—but some of the guys counted a $4,200 take from those performances as half their income for the year. Most of the time they worked no more than four shows in a month and tried to convince themselves they were doing the right thing.

"It had to be a big eye-opener for them, actually going out and doing stuff on the road," says Gene Johnson, a touring veteran who would meet—and join—the River Boys two years later. "You're not in that controlled environment anymore. You're goin' out and you're playin', it's costing you money now to get to shows, you don't have a guaranteed audience sittin' there. You actually have to draw them in or be playing with somebody that does. That scares away a lot of pickers right there. They changed a lot of pickers right in that time period. It's not quite as easy as it looks."

RESTLESS HEART'S ENCOURAGING SUCCESS

The success of another group, Restless Heart, gave the River Boys at least some hope that they could make the transition from Opryland to viable band. Restless Heart made its initial entry on the *Billboard* country chart during the first month of 1985, and by the end of the year, the band had landed two singles in the Top 10 and another in the Top 25. Two of the band's members—guitarist Greg Jennings and bass player Paul Gregg, the brother of the River Boys' Danny Gregg—were Opryland graduates.

Their producer, Tim DuBois, further cemented Restless Heart's connection to the park's corporate structure. His wife, Cee Cee, had been a background singer on one of the TNN shows with Paul Gregg and the River Boys' Matt Davenport. It was a small consolation, however. Restless Heart publicly glossed over its ties to the theme park, and only a couple of its members had worked at Opryland—not the entire band.

STAR SEARCH

The record labels weren't calling, but Hollywood did. *Star Search*, the same show that had provided a platform for former member Ty

Herndon, gave the Tennessee River Boys a slot in one of its episodes. The Boys had seen some of the bands that had competed in previous installments, and they were convinced they could place high with their performances. They were told to bring at least four stage outfits apiece, and the production crew seemed to think they'd move up the ladder fairly easily.

They didn't. Performing "Take Me to the River," they lost in the first round, adding to the sense of rejection they were feeling in other quarters.

"That was a really tough night," Marty says. "I remember sittin' in the hotel room on the bed, with the whole band, beatin' my head up against the wall—'I'm quittin' this business, it's stupid!' It was crushing."

FAMILY LIFE

Most of the group was married. Most were also purposely not having any babies. They couldn't afford them and couldn't afford the distraction from their career, unfruitful though it was.

Dan—whose wife, Wendee, worked on a show on Opryland's *General Jackson* showboat—was one of the few River Boys who looked after a child. Other than teaching some piano lessons and playing the scattered River Boys shows, Dan had no work, so he started most days by putting his son, Ben—who was eighteen months old as 1986 opened—in a wind-up swing set to keep the boy occupied while Dad practiced. After lunch Dan would take his son for a walk down Graycroft Avenue in Madison or run errands in the family's lone car, then tuck Ben in for a nap while he practiced again in the afternoon.

"I remember bein' in the car and I didn't want him to be asleep," Dan says. "I needed him to sleep at home so I could practice, so I'd start talkin' real loud. This is when he was one or two, so he might not understand what I was saying, but I'd be talkin' real loud and I remember him lookin' at me

Ben Truman–13 months old

like, *What are you doin'? I'm tryin' to go to sleep!* And I'd keep him awake all the way home so he'd go to sleep when I got home and I could practice."

DRUMMER LOST AND FOUND

Without Opryland supplying a regular check, the mix of nonpaying practices, relentless bills, and dependent families started to take its toll on the River Boys roster. The first casualty was J. J., the drummer.

"He got all sideways," Marty notes. "I don't really know why, but he was disenchanted with what we were doin'. There wasn't much money involved in it, so he quit."

They rounded up a few prospects and held auditions at Danny's home in a Donelson duplex. None of them quite fit the bill. But another Opryland drummer, Suzanne Elmer, thought she might have a solution for them. In addition to playing at the theme park, she also held down a night job in Jim

Vest's band at Faron Young's Country Junction, a club on Printers Alley. The musicians at the Alley's watering holes kept tabs on the talent at the other venues, too, and she knew of a drummer named Brian Prout, who worked with a band called Heartbreak Mountain at the Western Room.

© 1983–84 Brian Rawlings

Left to right: Jimmy Olander, Brian Prout, Marty Roe, Matt Davenport, Danny Gregg, Dan Truman

The River Boys set up a second day of auditions with several drummers, but thanks to Suzanne's recommendation, they were most interested in Brian. He had just turned thirty and felt he needed to find another outlet if he ever hoped to escape the club circuit. The Tennessee River Boys were mostly still in their twenties, with big-time aspirations. They were opening shows for name acts and appearing every once in a while on TV. The group had more promise than the Western Room, even if the River Boys did have that "Opryland reputation."

"There was a cheesy factor that I wasn't entirely comfortable with," Brian recalls. "But I saw something in the Tennessee River Boys that was different than any other band I'd been in: a combination of great talent, desire, commitment to each other, stability in a personal life—Dan was married, Marty was married, Jimmy was married."

Jimmy's membership came as a surprise to Brian. The two had met when Jimmy played in another Printers Alley club with a band called Sis, built around a pair of sisters from Washington State. Brian also knew Barbara Green, who was in the background when Jimmy opened the door at the audition. He *didn't* know Barb was Jimmy's wife. It was a bit awkward.

"There was never anything between us," Brian laughs, "but she was a barfly."

Her attendance at the audition was only a temporary distraction. Brian quickly focused on the business at hand, set up his drum kit, and started playing with the Tennessee River Boys.

"There was, hands down, no doubt that Brian was the best drummer," Marty remembers. "First of all, he'd listened to the tapes we'd sent him. Second of all, he really listened to us. He was, and [still is], the most musical drummer that I've ever played with. A lot of drummers, they just lay down a groove and you plug 'em in: *I'm drivin' a train, here we go, this is it.* They play great stuff, but it's like they're kinda in their own little world and not payin' attention to what everybody else is playing. Brian's paying attention. If Jimmy hits a lick and it happens more than twice or whatever, he'll inflect that on the drums. Vocal inflections—he ends up accentuating some of that stuff. I've always loved that about what he does, and he did that that day."

"It didn't even take one song," Dan says. "Before [Brian] finished the song, I was like, *This is the guy.*"

Brian not only had a big drum sound, he also talked loud and had a quip or an observation for just about any direction the conversation went.

"He definitely had that used-car-salesman vibe," Dan chuckles, "but he was the drummer if we were gonna get the best."

The Tennessee River Boys offered him the job that day, and Brian said yes before he left Danny's house. He wasn't entirely impressed with the band musically—"It was a little vanilla for my tastes," he concedes—but he thought it had more potential than anything he was doing on Printers Alley.

"They were young, good-looking guys," he reasons, "and I still had a bit of a look goin' for myself back then. And I had learned in my time in Nashville that music is a visually driven medium. At the end of the day, people hear with their eyes."

Brian left his drum set at Danny's house, and the band practiced two or three times for several weeks before they set off in a van, pulling a trailer, for Brian's first official gig in Pampa, Texas, during February 1986. It took at least fifteen hours each way, with a hotel stop in Oklahoma City. The gig paid all of $140—a lot of driving, a lot of time invested, relatively little pay.

LINEUP CHANGES

Saddled with such low compensation, the River Boys' lineup continued to evolve. Steel player Mel Deal turned in his resignation. Instead of replacing him, they allowed the band to shrink from seven players to six, making what little money came in stretch a little further.

Brian, as the newest face in the band, was unfettered by the River Boys' history, and he was already beginning to wonder if the lineup was structured correctly. Danny and Matt might have been the founders, but he was more intrigued by Marty as a vocalist. Being the new guy, Brian kept his opinion to himself.

"Danny had a way of warming up to a crowd that I just found fascinating," Brian recalls. "He was the consummate showman, and maybe

Fall of 1986. Left to right: Jimmy Olander, Marty Roe, Brian Prout, Danny Gregg, Dan Truman, Matt Davenport

that was his strength versus his vocal capacity. He was good, don't take me wrong, but through the course of the show, Danny would do most of the lead singin', and Matt would do a couple of songs, and then Marty did a couple. And Marty did a song written by Dobie Gray, called 'If I Ever Needed You, I Need You Now.' It was a big, '80s-power-ballad type thing, and gosh, I just couldn't wait to get to that song to hear Marty Roe sing that song.

"I was like, *Dad gum, this is the lead singer of this group.* Danny was the personality, no doubt, and the only time Marty participated in communicating with the crowd was when the three of them were doing their little skits back and forth that came from Opryland."

Because he kept that observation to himself, Brian was unaware that at least one of his fellow River Boys had briefly considered that same idea.

"I was in the front of our little converted bread truck [one time], and Marty was singing to himself as he was driving," Jimmy says. "He had a character to his voice that sounded like a commercial country singer. He was actually more country than the other two guys. Matt Davenport had this smooth baritone. It was rich, Jim Reeves-ey, but no character. Marty's got that little hick [flair]. There's more air in the voice, and it had a little bit more character to it."

First tour bus. "Back then the Eagle was the bus to have . . . we called it the 'Wounded Eagle.' It broke down *all* the time! It was awful." —Brian

Marty, however, also had self-esteem problems. Danny was Mr. Charisma, Matt had a rock-solid confidence, and Jimmy couldn't picture Marty taking command from them on stage.

🎵

But self-esteem issues were the least of the troubles the band members were facing. Jimmy, who had originally joined the band for financial reasons, felt an even greater strain on his wallet—and his pride—after he and his wife wrecked two vehicles. He had pulled his restored 1953 GMC pickup into traffic in front of his house on Nashville's Blair Boulevard and got hit by a Fiat. His wife, Barbara, had likewise slammed a car into a tree. Jimmy's dad was now shelling out money to help them get back on their feet. The marriage had never really gelled. After about five years together, Jimmy and Barbara had had enough and divorced.

Dan and Wendee couldn't afford health insurance and had piled up a load of medical expenses. They owed doctors somewhere around fourteen thousand dollars—more than the couple was bringing home annually—and by the beginning of 1987, Wendee was pregnant again. She took their son, Ben, back to Utah to live with her parents until the delivery. And Dan hopscotched between several sets of friends who let him stay at their homes while he worked through their debt.

"I kinda leeched off of people, [including] Marty and Robin," Dan confesses. "No one ever charged me. So we were savin' rent, [and] the utilities and the extras that come with that, and I would sock anything I made back into these medical bills. I got on a payment plan and doubled up on 'em, and paid it off in about three years."

The Trumans' separation was eased by one of the Tennessee River Boys' few benefits. The group played periodic corporate events for Northwest Airlines, and part of the compensation came in free round-trip tickets. A Northwest gig emerged about every six or eight weeks, and each time, Dan would use his ticket to visit the family in Utah for a couple of weeks. Then it was back to Tennessee, where he'd stay at a friend's house, rehearse, work, and wait for the next Northwest corporate booking.

On the return trips, he'd bring preserves for Marty and Robin in lieu of rent money.

"That was a big joke between Marty and I," Dan says. "Wendee and her mom, they were always [canning] jams and jellies, so I would always bring a stash in my carry-on bag. So we always had two or three jars in their fridge. Robin was never—and still isn't—much of a cook, and so every night, Marty and I were watching TV, eatin' toast and jelly."

Dan might have made do, but Danny Gregg could no longer hang. He was a little older than the rest of the band, had stowed away some

Photograph by G. Michael Allen

Tennessee River Boys promo picture 1987. *Back:* Jimmy Olander, Danny Gregg, Dan Truman, Matt Davenport *Front:* Marty Roe, Brian Prout

cash when he cohosted the TNN show a few years before, but was tired of eating through his savings.

Touring, at least the way the Tennessee River Boys did it, was also harder on Danny than the rest of the crew. He had had a serious illness in his teens, and as a result he maintained an organic diet and went through extreme rituals to avoid germs in public places. Eating in fast-food joints and using gas-station restrooms didn't suit him.

"Bein' out on the road at that level, we didn't have the extra coolness of a bus," Dan says. "We were in a funky converted truck. We did a year of that. Even though it was clubs and shows with Mel McDaniel and Ronnie McDowell and those guys, he [Danny Gregg] was pretty much over it. He couldn't take the intensity of that. I think if we had got a record deal—because it's so different at the level we're at now, you know, you have people cater to you and the bus and everything—he might have hung. But he just couldn't handle that."

Danny's departure was a major blow. He sang the bulk of the lead vocals and had a rapport with the audience that was irreplaceable. Even with Matt and Marty still on board, the band harbored doubts that it could survive the loss.

"I was really disappointed 'cause he was a friend and a leader, and he had so much charisma," Dan explains. "I remember we did this Elk's Lodge down in Florida, Danny turned around to us and goes, 'Plan B.' And I remember the first time I heard that, turning around to the drummer: 'Plan B?' He goes, 'Crowd agitation.' If the response wasn't great, he'd turn to crowd agitation. Danny could do it big-time. He was like Don Rickles in this strawberry-blond smile. He would start [jabbing at] people in the audience. It was hilarious."

As they'd done when Mel Deal quit, the Tennessee River Boys initially tried to get by with one less musician. Matt assumed the lead vocal position, with Marty taking a small share of the songs and providing the high harmony. They needed another voice for the baritone parts, and they tried all three remaining players—Jimmy, Dan, and Brian—deciding Brian should take a Don Henley role and sing from the drum kit.

That lasted only a few shows before they agreed they indeed needed to replace Danny. Matt would remain the front man, and they'd find a multi-instrumentalist to sing baritone.

Gene Johnson

The River Boys auditioned a number of musicians. But one who stood out was a referral Jimmy got through stand-up bass player Mark Schatz.

"I've got this friend of mine," Mark told Jimmy, "really good musician, really good singer. He's mostly doin' cabinet work and doing woodworking, and it's a crying shame. He needs to be playing [regularly]. I don't know if he would be into this or not. His name's Gene Johnson."

Jimmy's ears perked up. As a kid in Michigan, he'd persuaded his father to take him to a club called the Raven Gallery to see Eddie Adcock's

Photograph by G. Michael Allen

Tennessee River Boys, 1987. *Left to right:* Marty Roe, Gene Johnson, Matt Davenport, Brian Prout, Dan Truman, Jimmy Olander.

bluegrass band, IInd Generation, which featured a mandolin player named Gene Johnson. Was this the same guy?

"Gene played really smooth, really intelligent mandolin," Jimmy says. "It wasn't Bill Monroe, I'm-crankin'-away-on-two-strings, rural, lonesome stuff. It was technically really well done. And I had his records."

Gene was out of town when Jimmy placed the call, so Jimmy chatted a bit with June Johnson, who took down the number with a note for her husband to call about an audition with the Tennessee River Boys.

Gene ignored the message. He'd moved to Nashville twenty months before in an attempt to get out of bluegrass and get into country, which promised a better income. He'd played with some significant bluegrass musicians—including Eddie Adcock and J. D. Crowe. He'd never heard of the Tennessee River Boys, but with that name, the group had to be bluegrass. If he was going to bite the bullet and go back to that world, he'd do it with an act people knew.

Photo by Pat Corey

II Generation at a bluegrass festival in 1973. *Left to right:* Jeff Wisor, Gene Johnson, Eddie Adcock.

Jimmy called again. He made it clear that he was a fan and insisted the River Boys were a country band. He told Gene about the Opryland history—not a strong sales point—but Gene auditioned anyway.

"I'd been there and seen some of the shows at the park," Gene says, "and they all had a certain typical staged imitation thing usually goin' on. I almost cringed a little bit when he said that, but the fact that they were off and starting to play on the road, I thought, *Well, let's go up and sit in and see what it sounds like.*"

The audition was set at the home of the drummer, Brian, who had recently married another drummer, Nancy Given, who was part of Wild Rose, an all-female band. Jimmy, who'd so admired Gene as a kid, found it surreal to suddenly audition one of his heroes. The rest of the River Boys were unfamiliar with Gene. They'd been told about his history, but since they had no bluegrass background, his resume meant little to them.

In the middle of the audition, Pam Gadd—the lead vocalist for Wild Rose—wandered into the living room and asked for Gene's autograph. That was just weird—people who are significant enough to sign autographs aren't usually required to audition.

"I remember the look on Marty and Matt's faces," Gene laughs, "kinda goin', *Who is this guy?*"

The better question was what to do with him.

"We weren't looking for a mandolin player, and we weren't looking for a tenor," Marty says.

Gene wasn't looking to sing baritone either. And when one of the River Boys said the singers in the group had always traded off the lead vocals and tenor parts—well, Gene certainly wasn't looking for that.

Renee Behrman-Greiman Courtesy of Modern Management

Brian's former home on McGavock Pike. "We rehearsed in the basement and in the winter months we would disconnect the hose from the dryer and use that to heat the room." —Brian

"I come from the bluegrass field where one thing you knew for sure is you tried to keep your harmonies the same," he explains. "If you've got somebody that's got a good tenor voice, you have him sing tenor. It gives you a sound, something that's different from somebody else. You definitely don't wanna just keep switchin' all the harmonies. I think that was just having come out of the park, they weren't thinking on a professional level with everything yet."

Gene did see some other qualities when they played together, though, and that was enough for him to give them a tentative thumbs-up.

"I was very impressed with Jimmy and very impressed with Dan, impressed with Brian," Gene reflects. "Matt seemed to be a fine bass player, you know. Marty couldn't play rhythm very well, but he sang well, so my first impression of 'em was, *Well, pretty talented bunch of guys.*

"So I thought, *I'll play some with 'em. I don't have anything else pressing. It's in my best interest to pick up a few dollars here, if I can pick up a few dollars, and we'll see how things work out.*"

From the River Boys' perspective, Gene might have been a Rolling

Stones–type solution: you can't always get what you want. They did get what they needed.

"Even though I thought it was the end of the world when we lost Danny Gregg," Dan says, "Gene was a part of the puzzle that was missing. That harmony made all the difference in the world for us."

Their new mandolin player made his debut with the Tennessee River Boys during a test run in Clewiston, Florida, on May 4, 1987. The next day they played Jekyll Island, Georgia, and tossed him three hundred dollars for his efforts. They also made Gene a full-time member, commencing with a three-week stint at the Landmark Hotel in Las Vegas.

His addition created some apprehension for Marty. Matt, one of the original members, was now the official lead singer. Marty had been bumped from the easily distinguished high-tenor harmonies to the lower voice in the triad. He had the second longest tenure in the Tennessee River Boys, yet his place in the creative pecking order—from the outside, anyway—had dropped.

"I was somewhat resistant," Marty admits, "'cause I loved singin' that high-harmony part, you know. I got to sing lead on one or two songs, but I [had been] mostly singin' high harmony and playin' acoustic. I really didn't have a huge role in the band, to be honest. I was actually honored to be playin' with them. All of these guys are better musicians than I am, so I was just kind of tryin' to hang on to my job—what little job I had."

WHO IS IN CHARGE?

Things seemed to be stabilizing in the band, even if the guys continued to struggle financially. Gene, who was thirty-seven, had been married to June for fourteen years, and they had two children. Brian and Marty were each married. Jimmy reveled in life after his divorce. And Wendee delivered the Trumans' second son, Chad, in September 1987 and moved back to Tennessee.

Chad (1 year), Dan, Ben (4 years)

Most of the guys found outside sources for additional income. Gene continued his carpentry, Jimmy and Marty mowed lawns, and Brian drove tourists around in a bus to see the homes of the stars.

Despite the stability, however, the River Boys developed some tension over ownership. Matt and Marty, as the senior members, served as leaders, and since Marty invariably deferred to his partner, that left Matt in charge. As they continued to contemplate a recording deal, the guys began debating what percentage of the group each member owned. Matt insisted his and Marty's tenure entitled them to a larger share of any income. The rest of the band thought the income should be split evenly. And Marty was siding with them.

"It's like Matt and I are owners of nothing if these guys don't stay," Marty shrugs. "So it was just the right thing to do. I was glad to do it, and it made perfect sense. We were basically a six-way partnership anyhow; we just needed to make it that way officially."

Photograph by G. Michael Allen.

The Tennesee River Boys before Dana Williams joined the band, 1987.
Left to right: Matt Davenport, Brian, Marty, Dan, Gene, Jimmy.

Keith Stegall's Contribution

The partnership would change even more when they caught the atten-tion of singer-songwriter Keith Stegall in 1988. After writing jazz singer Al Jarreau's lone Top 10 pop hit "We're in This Love Together" in 1981, Keith had secured three Top 20 singles as a country artist in the mid-'80s. He'd also written several other songs that had received huge radio play, including Glen Campbell's "A Lady Like You" and Mickey Gilley's "Lonely Nights."

Keith was looking to become a producer and was working with a shy, lanky singer-songwriter named Alan Jackson. Keith also had worked out a deal with his publishing company in which he could produce some material on the Tennessee River Boys and get demos made for some of his songs at the same time. So he took them into the studio to see what they could develop.

Matt's position as the lead singer and bass player posed a technical problem. His voice and his instrument needed to be on separate tracks; if he recorded both simultaneously, Keith would never be able to untangle them in the control room. The solution was easy: Marty would sing "scratch" vocals while Matt laid down the bass part at the same time the other musicians recorded their tracks. They could go in later and replace Marty's voice with Matt's.

Working with those tracks, Keith heard Marty delivering the songs that Matt normally sang with a different edge. After the band went home one night, Keith called several members to float an idea. He was convinced that if the River Boys were going to make it commercially, they needed Marty in the lead slot.

It wasn't the first time anyone had thought about giving Marty the chance to lead. Brian had reached that conclusion soon after joining. Jimmy thought Marty had the chops for the job, but not necessarily the bravado. Gene, the newcomer, had already recognized that Marty had more character as a vocalist. And Dan had long felt Marty was a more powerful, more expressive singer. Yet no one had ever discussed it. Matt was a likable guy, certainly capable as a singer, and he had a much bigger personality than Marty. He'd kind of risen to lead the pack, and no one had thought to challenge the status quo.

"Matt is such a great songwriter, and he's such a great showman," Dan says. "To me, there was still that perception that he was the guy that hired me."

Keith talked it over with the guys in a band meeting, and Matt reluctantly accepted what certainly felt like a demotion. They made the demos and shopped them around town again, and the guys had such a positive feeling about their potential that Jimmy—struggling though he was—turned down a lucrative gig.

Lee Greenwood, who'd slipped "God Bless the U.S.A." into a string of nineteen Top 10 hits since 1981, offered him a job as the guitarist in his road band. Jimmy told Lee he was optimistic the River Boys could land a deal and that if they did, he wouldn't be able to finish the tour. Lee thanked him for his honesty and moved on.

Shopping Around and Hangin' On

Keith took the River Boys demo around town, and the feedback was better than when Snuffy Miller had tried several years earlier. Jim Ed Norman, still at Warner Bros., was particularly impressed with the progress they'd made but didn't have room for them on his roster.

So the guys continued their outside jobs. One day, Brian was giving yet another bus tour of the homes of the stars and encountered an ironic sight: just weeks after Jimmy had passed on the road job, he was out cutting grass for the man he'd turned down, Lee Greenwood.

At the end of '88, the River Boys had a two-week engagement at Le Louisiane in Quebec, the perfect opportunity for Marty and Matt to adjust to their new roles. Matt still introduced some of the songs and sang lead a bit, but they had literally swapped positions.

"I was a nervous wreck," Marty says. "I hadn't really given a whole lot of thought about being put in that [front man] position, so it was a little overwhelming for me. But we made it through that, and everybody seemed to think it went well and that was the path."

But maybe not the path for everyone. Matt had children to feed, and his wife was unhappy that he was chasing this music dream instead of working a more standard job. He had envisioned being a 50 percent owner of a band in which he sang lead. Now he had one-sixth partnership in a group where he sang the low harmonies.

"I'm home maybe a day or two, and Matt calls me," Marty recalls. "It's the end of the year, we don't have any work, probably through January or whatever. Matt told me—and this is a quote—that 'the Lord is leading me to leave the band.'"

Matt was gone.

While the calendar was full of holes, the River Boys had one attractive date on the books: a January 23 appearance on Ralph Emery's TNN talk show *Nashville Now.*

They needed a replacement, and they needed him quick. And this time they couldn't be flexible the way they had been when Gene came on board: the new guy needed to sing the third harmony part and play bass.

They flirted with Alan LaBeouf, who had just left Baillie & the Boys, a group that had gone Top 10 with the radio-friendly "Oh Heart" and "Long Shot." Alan, who had played Paul McCartney in a Broadway production of *Beatlemania,* was initially interested but canceled his audition when his plate filled up. He ultimately returned to work in Beatles tribute shows.

Gene also approached Jeff Amiot, who'd played bass in a couple of his earlier bluegrass groups. Jeff was working at a hospital in New York State and valued having a reliable paycheck. He declined the offer too.

Dana Williams

Jimmy put in a call to Dana Williams, the former Jimmy C. Newman sideman who used to watch the original version of the River Boys when Ty Herndon—not Marty—sang most of the lead parts. When Jimmy did his first Opryland stint as a member of the *Country Music USA* cast, he had become acquainted with Dana, and they'd periodically run into each other on the Nashville club circuit.

Jimmy was rather sheepish during the call, still feeling some embarrassment about working with a band best known for its theme-park connection. But he asked Dana to audition anyway.

"I thought it was gonna be way beneath him," Jimmy says. "But he's like, 'Dude, I *love* the Tennessee River Boys! I used to see 'em all the time out there at the park. I love them. When you want me to come?'"

They ended up talking for a couple of hours that day, and Dana found himself making excuses when he told his wife, Lisa, he had an audition. After a weary decade of playing nightclubs and backing up Grand Ole Opry performers, he had brought home an application to attend electronics school.

She didn't need to worry, he promised. He was done with this music thing. Jimmy was an old friend and auditions never lead anywhere. ("If you get 'auditioned,' that's the first breath of death for that gig," Dana still maintains.)

"I'm not gonna get sucked in now," Dana told her.

Still, there was something different about this band.

"I had been looking from all of my experience [for] someone I could go on the road with that nobody's doin' drugs, nobody drinks, and there wasn't any issue like that," Dana says. "And when I get this call from Jimmy, I remember tellin' my wife at the time, 'I don't know *why* I feel I need to do this, but I just feel like I need to go and do this and see what happens. I don't have a clue why. They don't have one thing to offer anybody. I will say it would be kinda cool to do that TV show.' And that was the main reason—they had this TV show and, yeah, it'd kinda be cool to be on that."

The audition in Brian's garage was less than comfortable. It was the dead of winter, so they turned on the clothes dryer and left the door open to heat the room. Just one lightbulb hung from the ceiling, and they positioned Dana under it "interrogation style," as Marty says.

"The package that showed up to audition was the old Dana Williams that was heavy [with a] really, really full, bushy beard," Jimmy says, "this big, unkept [guy] with the Johnny Lee hat and the calico shirt. It was that guy showin' up for the Tennessee River Boys, [who had been] pretty boys out at Opryland doing a six-piece thing where everybody had to look stylish somewhat."

Jimmy didn't know how his old friend would go over. But they'd already heard plenty of bad auditions. They had tried out a wannabe from Belmont College on a peaceful, easy mid-tempo number, and the kid started thumping the strings like a heavy-metal bassist. That clearly wouldn't work. Other guys could play the bass parts but were shaky on the vocals.

Dana had a bit of an attitude about auditioning, but when it came time to do the job, he sailed through the music—especially on the vocals. Dana had learned harmony through his relationship with his uncles, the Osborne Brothers, best known for the bluegrass classic "Rocky Top." His vocal approach fit perfectly with Gene's bluegrass background, and both of them meshed well with Marty's twang.

"I gotta say, man, there was kind of an instant thing," Dana reflects. "You could hear it. It just instantly—*shoomp*—came together."

Because of Dana's attitude and his presentation, they hesitated. There was another guy who tried out who was almost as good, and he had a lot less of an attitude. They decided to bring both players back for a second audition.

Photo by Amy Carraway

October 19, 1991, Paducah, Kentucky. *L to r:* Gene, Dana, Marty. "So much hair, so little space." —Jimmy

Dana groused about that, too, but he came back. And in addition to running through songs they'd asked him to learn, they tested him on a few they hadn't assigned him. He fell into the right harmonies automatically.

"He wouldn't even know these songs—and, to this day, he still doesn't," Jimmy laughs. "Even now, there's songs that we do where he won't sing all the consonants, but he gets the vowels right and he blends. Marty accuses him of this: 'You don't even know the words!' But it still sounds good."

Dana was hired. Within short order, he'd join them on *Nashville Now*. And they hoped he'd stay as they plowed forward with their pursuit of a recording contract. Time, it seemed, was running out. Wendee Truman had grown tired of feeding a family of four on twelve thousand dollars a year. Dan had promised he'd give it just one more year. Marty had determined—much like Alabama's Randy Owen had done a decade before—that he would quit if he hadn't made it by age thirty. That deadline was twenty months away.

Photo by Brannin Tanaka

Dollywood at Pigeon Forge. *Left to right:* **Dan, Jimmy, Dana, Brian, Marty, Gene**

They were long gone from the theme park. The Tennessee River Boys were uncertain how much longer they could continue the ride. But they would take it together. The six musicians had come from five different states and very different backgrounds, but they shared a common bond. They each wanted to be part of a successful *band*—an aspiration that cut against the grain in country music.

Solo artists can make decisions—about songs, about tours, about managers—in a snap. A band has an extra layer of friction: it requires extra meetings, lots of communication, and an uncommon willingness to sacrifice personal goals for the good of the team.

Left to right: Dan, Gene, Dana, Marty, Jimmy, and Brian, singing the National Anthem at the Braves game, July 1995. "There's nothing like acid washed jeans and big hair to prove we were fashion forward in the early 90's . . . *not!*" —Jimmy

July 1995. "Atlanta Braves vs. Pittsburg Pirates . . . this was the year the Braves ended up going to the World Series." —Brian

Finding *six* guys with those personal skills? That's a feat. Each of the River Boys had that kind of dedication, though they came to it in different ways.

chapter 3

MARTY ROE

Russ Harrington

hen Timothy Martin Roe was born, the occasion had loose connections to his future occupation as a singer, though no one knew his destiny at the time.

His mother, Roberta—or Bertie, as she was best known—was the daughter of a coal miner in eastern Kentucky, who'd worked in the same Van Lear mines as Loretta Lynn's daddy. Bertie had met the new baby's father, Zane Roe, in the mid-1950s when he attended Morehead State. Zane had a radio show during his college days, and another kid named Tom Hall read the commercials on the air.

Loretta, destined to become a member of the Country Music Hall of Fame, made her Grand Ole Opry debut in October 1960, when Bertie was seven months pregnant with Marty. Tom Hall would later add the middle initial "T" after moving to Nashville, becoming Tom T. Hall, writing songs for Jimmy C. Newman's publishing company, and eventually building a career also worthy of Country Music Hall of Fame membership.

When Marty—as most people referred to the baby—arrived in Lebanon, Ohio, on December 28, 1960, his middle name was a nod to Marty Robbins, Zane's favorite singer. The smooth-voiced Robbins had ridden through the year with a couple of classic country recordings—"El

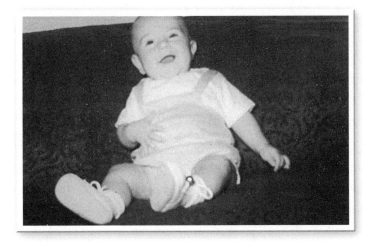

"Summer of '61. Fat boy . . . 25 pounds at 6 months old." —Marty

Paso" and "Big Iron"—and, just five days before the Roe kid's arrival, had recorded "Don't Worry," in which a problem with an amplifier led to the first fuzz-tone guitar ever used on a country record.

Loretta Lynn, Tom T. Hall, and Marty Robbins weren't necessarily precursors to Marty Roe's future, but they added an interesting twist to his debut, which was also connected to country's heart and soul through his family's working-class roots.

Marty's coal-mining grandfather was a large man—much like the character in Jimmy Dean's 1961 concoction, "Big Bad John." He stood six foot four inches, which made for severely cramped conditions when he went down into the deep, dark mines for his grueling twelve-hour shifts. Most veins were only thirty inches high—never more than forty-eight inches—so the workers spent large chunks of time on their stomachs, chipping away at the rock and creating an atmosphere of thick, sooty dust.

In the 1930s, he was a union organizer, taking a baseball bat and a pistol to work for safety's sake. He warned his sons—six boys total among his nine children—against the evils of the mine, and not one of them ever went down underground to make his living in coal. Despite that antagonism toward his work, he spent forty-two years on the job before a stroke put an end to his vocation. He died ten years later, in 1979, suffering from black lung and a heart condition that required surgery—an operation he declined.

"Open-heart surgery was a really new thing, and he wasn't goin' under the knife," Marty recalls. "They told him he had blockages and he needed bypasses, and he wouldn't do it. So he got up one morning, put his overalls on, laid down on the couch, wasn't feelin' really good, laid back, and 'see you later,' he was gone. Not a bad way to go."

Marty remembers him as a hero, a man who "lived large"—took his grandson hunting and fishing and played with him on the living room floor before Marty was old enough for school.

Marty's grandfather on the Roe side of the family was a farmer with a bent for old-fashioned values. He never owned a tractor, instead plowing his 140 acres with a mule team until he was ninety years old. They lived without electricity until sometime around World War II and never had air-conditioning or central heating. Even after Zane built him an indoor bathroom in the late 1960s, he still preferred using the outhouse. The family supplied most of its own needs right there on the farm, making a little money on the side from tobacco fields.

Marty, age 4, in front with cousin Wayne behind him. The horse belonged to Uncle Arville Short.

Marty's first Christmas.

"Scott (my brother) and I headed to church. It could be Easter Sunday . . . somewhere around '67 or '68." —Marty

He had a great deal of pride and refused to take part in the Social Security system, founded in the midst of the Great Depression when he was in his late forties. He never had one of those "ten-digit numbers"—he insisted on taking care of himself—and he never drew a dime from the government to make his way.

Bertie worked as a bank teller until Marty came along in 1960, four years after she'd married Zane. She stayed at home until Marty was a high school senior, then returned to the banking industry where she became a manager for twenty years before retiring.

Zane was primarily a schoolteacher, although he still did a little farming on a thirty-acre plot of land. He did whatever it took—a mail route, real estate, tax preparation, promotional merchandising (pens, calendars, etc.) for small businesses—to keep the family fed. In addition he began a forty-year tenure as an elder at the Church of Christ.

"It's Ozzie and Harriet," Marty assesses. "I kinda grew up in an ideal family situation. My parents loved one another. They both worked hard, and we didn't make a whole lot of money. We kept up with the Joneses as much as possible, but that's not what we were really about. I learned how to work with what you have and not be mad about what you don't have. That's just kinda how I grew up and was surprised later to find out that's not necessarily normal."

Zane had a band during his college years, and the little free time the family had often revolved around music.

"My dad's brother, Kurt, was a good mandolin player and he sang," Marty notes. "He had six kids—they all play and sing. My dad's side of the family, we all play music. If you didn't play an instrument and sing, then you were just a spectator when we got together."

Music was a lot more interesting than the daily chores. Marty got up early every morning to slop the hogs before school. After classes he went back to work on the farm, helping to plant, tend, and harvest the corn crop, which usually brought in about three thousand dollars every year. Marty was driving a tractor by the time he was ten or eleven—in fact, it was perfectly legal to take it out on the road at that age, even though he wasn't old enough to drive a car.

"Didn't like it," Marty says of the endless farm chores. "Hated it. Absolutely hated it at the time."

He loved music, though, and there was lots of it. He started playing trumpet in the fourth grade. The family had those group sing-alongs whenever they got together, and he took up singing at home while his dad played a Fender electric guitar. Indicative of his future job as a touring artist, the first song Marty learned to sing in its entirety was country, Merle Haggard's "The Fugitive." ("I'd like to settle down but they won't let me / A fugitive must be a rolling stone.")

Marty began playing guitar well enough to accompany himself, and Zane recognized his son's obvious abilities, though it took a lot of prodding to actually get the kid to sing in front of anyone.

"I'd hide from him when people would come over," Marty recalls. "He'd go, 'Hey, Marty, get your guitar and play us a song,' 'cause he was proud. I hated that, but the second I would actually do it, then it was like I'd play all night for you. I'd get through that little nervousness, and I'd be okay."

The Roes also began playing regularly at the Carter City Jamboree, a Saturday-night music event in a small town just north of Olive Hill, Kentucky. They put church pews in a run-down warehouse and attracted about two hundred people every weekend for three hours of music, with an intermission allowing folks to go outside and smoke a cigarette.

In that setting, Marty sang publicly for the first time with a band, delivering a Gordon Lightfoot song, "Ribbon of Darkness," that Marty Robbins had turned into a hit in 1965.

"It might as well have been the Grand Ole Opry to me," Marty reflects. "It was like, *Oh, my gosh, all these people come to see a show and I'm gonna get up there and play.*"

He apparently did well. The people started clapping along—a great response—but it completely shook Marty up. He lost his place in the music, forgot the words, then turned red from embarrassment. He might have even cried. He never quite finished the song. During the smoke break the adults kept egging him on, telling him they wanted to hear the whole thing. They promised not to clap, and during the second set he went ahead with it, navigating his way through "Ribbon" while the audience figuratively sat on its hands. By the time he finished, the applause was rampant, and Marty became a regular singer at the Jamboree.

Kay Jones, who lived near the Roes in Ohio, recruited Marty for some church-related musical ensembles she put together. One, the Dayton Youth Chorus, pulled together teens in the area to sing modern Christian songs. The other, a vocal quartet they called the Heavenly Bodies, included Kay's brother, Chris; J. T. Profitt; and Joe Bennie, who maintained a life-long friendship with Marty and would eventually become Diamond Rio's accountant.

Kay played a major role in a couple of events during 1974 that helped shape Marty's future. First, she convinced him to play a banquet for some older high school kids in the Columbus area. The Roes drove their son the eighty miles for the performance and a free meal, and Marty chipped in a thirty-minute solo set, singing "Take Me Home, Country Roads" and probably "We've Only Just Begun." Marty may have been a bit of a novelty that day.

"I was maybe five-foot-one," he says. "I wasn't much taller than the guitar. I know that these people were goin', *Wow, look at this little kid that plays and sings with guitar!*"

But the event made an impression. As usual, Marty was nervous when he started, but he grew more confident with each number. Afterward, Kay gave him fifty dollars for his time.

"You might as well have given me a thousand dollars," Marty says. "I'd been cuttin' grass, cuttin' lawns, and balin' hay—this guy paid me and a couple friends of mine a dollar a bale. The old bulb went on: *This is what I need to do right here. This is awesome.*"

That fall, Kay influenced Marty's life again when she took the chorus to Nashville, where they sang in suburban Smyrna and at the Granny White Church of Christ, on Granny White Pike near David Lipscomb University.

"I loved Nashville," he recalls. "The weather was pretty nice, and growin' up in Ohio was a little too cold for Mr. Roe. I was convinced, 'I'm goin' down there.' This is at thirteen years old, and I never wavered. I knew exactly where I wanted to be at that point."

"Me getting ready for Sunday school. Somewhere around 1972 . . . around 11 or 12 years old." —Marty

Marty's focus on music—and his ability with it—were strong enough that when his junior and senior years rolled around, he was able to keep his first-chair slot as a trumpet player in the concert band, even though he had to miss some of the rehearsals to make practice for football, where he played defensive end.

Jazz musician Chuck Mangione scored an instrumental hit in early 1978 with "Feels So Good," and Marty played flugelhorn—just like Chuck—in the school's jazz band. But he was mostly filling time until he could get off the farm and make his way to Music City.

"Marty Roe was watchin' the clock to turn eighteen," future band-mate Dana Williams says. "He's told me that many times. Soon as it hit, he was gone. And he came straight south."

Marty, age 15, Lebanon Warriors Defensive End.

There was one little hitch in that plan. Larry Gatlin and his brothers, Steve and Rudy, had gone into Nashville's Creative Workshop—a studio just two blocks from the Granny White Church of Christ, where Marty had previously sung—and recorded a dramatic, harmony-filled ballad called "I've Done Enough Dyin' Today." The song hit the *Billboard* charts in November 1978, just seven weeks before Marty turned eighteen, and Bertie flipped out when she heard it on their local country station.

She bought a copy of the single—something she almost never did—then brought it home for Marty to hear, telling him, "It sounds just like you." She was trying to encourage her son, but when Marty heard the similarities, her gesture had the opposite effect.

"I was depressed," he explains. "I went, 'Well, they've already got one of those. They probably don't need another one.'"

Despite his reservations, Marty did indeed head to Nashville after he

Marty's high school graduation, 1979. Marty with brother Scott.

completed high school. With his farm background, he thought he might end up a veterinarian, so he signed up for pre-med at David Lipscomb College and drove to town in a green 1972 Ford Pinto. He'd bought the car for $325 and worked with Zane to overhaul the engine and breathe new life into it.

Lipscomb was a jolt. When he arrived in town eager to start his adult journey, Marty saw a number of BMWs, a few Mercedes, and even an occasional Porsche in the parking lot. Those kinds of cars were practically nonexistent in rural Lebanon, Ohio, and the Lipscomb students who drove them often littered their conversations with topics that didn't seem particularly important to him.

"I was a fish out of water," he says. "These kids were dressed up. They were preppy, and they wore ties and penny loafers. And here I am in my tennis shoes and T-shirts, comin' from an Ohio hillbilly town. I didn't fit in."

But at least he was in Nashville. He was a short drive from Music Row, where all the record companies signed their Merle Haggards and their Larry Gatlins. He didn't know how to get in touch with the label people, but it didn't matter. They'd probably find him.

Marty quickly set about doing his music. Lipscomb had two choruses—an a cappella choir and the chorale—and he alternated between them, choosing his membership each semester based on which chorus had the most attractive destinations booked for its promotional trips. He also played in the Lipscomb coffeehouse and got noticed by the dean of students, who asked Marty to play on Lipscomb's behalf at a banquet a Christian school was holding in Columbia, Tennessee. The school paid Marty twenty dollars and a stack of Burger King scratch-off coupons that he dropped in the Pinto for future use.

He had one girlfriend during his first year or so at Lipscomb, and he was convinced she was *the one*. Instead, she was the one who "just stomped my heart flat," Marty says. The emotional damage was severe, but instead of retreating completely into his shell, he went the other direction and threw caution to the wind. He figured he couldn't be hurt much worse by anyone else, so he started asking out every pretty girl on campus. Marty got a number of dates that way. Sometimes it was a short night of boredom. In one instance there was no romantic spark, but he formed a long-term friendship with the girl.

Meanwhile, there was one blonde, Robin, he kept passing in the halls after a cappella chorus rehearsals, and it turned out that one of his friends, Mark Hayes, knew her. Marty prodded Mark to introduce them in the spring of 1981, and the three of them ditched class to see a Lipscomb baseball game, then split a hot-fudge cake and coffee at the Shoney's in Green Hills.

Things went well enough that Marty asked Robin to accompany him to church on Wednesday, and afterward he took her in the Pinto for dinner at a nice restaurant. To pass the time during the drive, she scratched off the Burger King coupons Marty had stashed in the car and discovered he had at least enough tickets for two free meals. When she spotted a BK sign, she convinced him they should have dinner there, proving she was—at the very least—practical.

He kissed her that night.

"There was really no magic there," he laughs, "and she says the same thing."

But they saw each other again, and again. And again. Within a month they were an item, and within two months they were engaged.

For Marty, who thought of his parents as Ozzie and Harriet, hearing Robin's history was an eye-opening experience. She was reluctant to tell him much at first, though she gradually began to reveal her story after she realized she could trust him. Her father had died of amyotrophic lateral sclerosis, often called Lou Gehrig's disease, about the time Robin started kindergarten. Her mother had been left on her own with few skills and no job or money. The courts split up Robin and her five brothers, and she lived with an aunt and uncle.

Despite a less-than-ideal upbringing, Robin had managed to build her social skills nicely. She even sang at the Lipscomb coffeehouse. Marty's self-confidence was admittedly shaky, but she had seen him perform. She believed he had talent and she had a way of instilling in him a little of that belief.

He couldn't afford a ring, but the engagement was on and it lasted nearly two years.

"I could be myself," he says. "I don't think I felt that way around any other girls before. It was just real fun, and a friendly relationship."

Robin quickly prodded Marty into considering Windsong. The group was a promotional ensemble for Lipscomb that performed primarily at high schools to recruit future students. Windsong members received a full-ride scholarship. If Robin could appreciate a free meal at Burger King, she certainly understood the value of a free education. She did some homework and got Marty set up for an audition. She also helped him prepare, encouraging him to do the Gatlin song "I've Done Enough Dyin' Today."

"I'd never auditioned in my life," Marty says. "I didn't know what an audition was, basically."

Marty, 22 years old, Opryland stage, 1982.

But he passed it and soon he had free tuition and some new musical friends, including a guitar player named Monty Powell.

Marty and Robin both got jobs at the Opryland theme park out on Briley Parkway. He helped tourists get in and out of the sky lift, and she worked the kiddie rides. Both of them could hear music from the Theater-by-the-Lake, where the *Country Music USA* show repeated multiple times every day. Somebody was singing Larry Gatlin & the Gatlin Brothers Band's "All the Gold in California," and Robin knew her fiancé was at least as good as that guy. Marty kind of thought so, too, but it was her enthusiasm—which included enough ambition to do all the legwork—that encouraged him to do the audition.

"If I never met her," Marty says, "I don't think I would be in the music business. I mean, she's fearless. That stuff—tryouts, auditions—all that kind of stuff, she researched what to do, and I just wasn't that way. I wanted to do it and I wanted to sing, but at that time I didn't have that kind of initiative to go find out how you do that."

In fact, Marty doubled up on auditions for Opryland's music productions. He went with Monty Powell and Windsong drummer Kip Rains to group auditions, then booked a separate solo audition where, once again, he trotted out "I've Done Enough Dyin' Today." In both instances he got callbacks, and it wasn't until his fourth time in front of the casting

Left to right: Steven, Marty. "Steven Curtis Chapman and I doing Flatt and Scruggs at Opryland. I'm Lester and he's Earl." —Marty

directors that they realized they'd seen a whole lot of Marty Roe. Monty got hired for the park's '50s rock 'n' roll show, and Marty was added to the cast of *Country Music USA*, where the producers scrapped "All the Gold" and had him sing "I've Done Enough Dyin'."

Money was still tight. The Opryland work was seasonal, and Robin had moved on to a job at a department store, Castner Knott. But her aunt and uncle were unable to pay for the wedding, so all their extra bucks went to finance their vows and a honeymoon. They were married December 11, 1982, at the West End Church of Christ, and went on a honeymoon to Gatlinburg until they'd depleted just about all their savings.

As the money ran out, they climbed into Marty's recently purchased lime-green '76 Mustang II grasping a twenty-dollar bill—their entire financial portfolio—then drove to Ohio to spend Christmas with his parents. After the holidays Zane loaned the newlyweds enough money to

Marty and Robin Roe, December 11, 1982,
West End Church of Christ.

make it back to Nashville, where Robin had a $125 paycheck waiting, and they began life together in Nashville.

Monty got married about the same time, and the two couples lived across the street from each other on Belvedere, a two-block road that practically emptied into the Lipscomb campus. Marty and Robin couldn't afford to be in school concurrently, so she worked full-time at Castner Knott while he finished his studies. Marty had dropped pre-med to major in business administration, and they agreed to reverse roles later while she completed her degree.

It soon became clear to Marty that Opryland's management liked him. Leslie Uggams and Peter Marshall hosted a daytime show in 1983 called *Fantasy*, in which ordinary people had dreams fulfilled. NBC producers approached Opryland about supplying a singer for one installment, and they offered up Marty, who was flown out to Los Angeles to shoot the episode.

Marty was clueless. Having never been on an airplane, he was confused when he had to make a connecting flight; but he eventually landed at LAX with instructions to find a specific cab and take it to Burbank. Finding the right cab was, in itself, an adventure. Once he got situated in the backseat, the driver headed north on the 405 freeway, and Marty started watching the meter tick ever higher.

"It's sixty dollars for the cab ride," he remembers. "I got twenty dollars in my pocket, man. I got nothin'. It's just rackin' up. It's up to forty dollars, and the whole time, I'm freakin' out. I do not have the money to pay this guy. I decided not to tell him. I'm gonna get to where we're goin' before I tell him. And so we get there, and I said, 'Man, I don't think I have money—' 'Oh no, NBC's payin' it. You just sign this.' And he had a sheet to sign. I didn't know anything about that stuff."

Marty checked into his hotel and waited for the phone to ring. In the meantime, he stared out the window at the hills, trying to discern why it all seemed like a déjà vu moment when he'd never been in California before. Why did those hills look so familiar?

He suddenly had this image of helicopters rising over the horizon, and he recognized that he'd seen a similar picture almost weekly on TV.

"*M*A*S*H!*" he laughs. "Go figure! They shoot *M*A*S*H* out here! It was that terrain."

Marty sang a Ronnie Milsap song, "Stranger in My House," on *Fantasy* and went with his handler, Jane Beber, to a birthday party for a member of the *CHiPs* production crew. The party was filled with actors his age, all good-looking and friendly, chatting about sports or pop culture or whatever was newsworthy at the time.

Outside of Jane, only one other woman was at the party, a beautiful blonde who had just been on the cover of *Seventeen* magazine. Marty struck up a conversation—she was still in high school; her parents had moved to L.A. so she could start her modeling career. It was odd to Marty. He was married—nothing was going to develop there—but he was the only guy who spent much time talking with her.

"I'm thinkin', *Hey, man, I'm doin' pretty good here with this chick,*" Marty recalls. "So we finally leave, and Jane Beber goes, 'Man, all those guys are all askin' about you, wantin' to know who you were.' I said, 'Oh really?' She said, 'Oh yeah, they're all gay.' 'Oh really. No wonder I was doin' so good with that chick!'"

"I was just green," Marty laughs, "wet behind the ears."

Opryland had delivered a rather strange experience. But it gave him a taste of some of the things he wanted—a chance to sing on TV and some travel. He didn't realize at the time just how significant Opryland would be for his future.

The Tennessee River Boys would soon come calling, and Marty would be on his way.

chapter 4

DAN TRUMAN

Russ Harrington

*T*he lyrics of some prominent country songs—Brooks & Dunn's "Hard Workin' Man," in particular—celebrate men who make their living with their hands. The people who make the music likewise depend on their hands, and the wise ones go to great lengths to protect them.

Such is the case for piano player Dan Truman, who has been careful about his fingers ever since his youth, guided by his father's instructions. The elder Truman, Delmont, was the son of a rancher and had to run some of his cattle to Los Angeles during the 1950s. Jumping out of the truck during a stop in Baker, California, he grabbed at a wooden slat on the truck bed to brace himself, but as he hopped down his wedding ring caught on a nail. He made it to the ground, but his ring finger was freakishly ripped out in the process.

That kind of accident seems to run in the Truman family: one of Delmont's uncles lost a finger to a firecracker; another lost three fingers in a lawnmower accident. So when Dan wanted a class ring in high school, his father balked: "You're gonna play piano. Let's don't mess with your fingers."

Dan's relationship to the keyboard can be traced directly to his family. His mother, Karol K. Truman, was an accomplished classical pianist and an instructor in the Dixie Community College Music Department in St. George, Utah, the small town where Dan was born August 29, 1956. She also taught private lessons at the Truman home.

Delmont, in addition to his ranching, sang publicly several times a week, providing a strong musical foundation around the house.

"My dad is a really good singer, baritone—kind of a big, powerful, Robert Goulet–type of voice—and so my folks were always doin' stuff," Dan says. "He's a real dynamic kind of guy, fun guy, so he was always singing—I mean *always* singing. So my house was just filled with music, and I just wanted to learn to play the piano."

His mother's employment at the college's music school gave her prestige in town among piano instructors, but she declined to give

Dan at 4 years old

Flagstaff, Arizona. "Mom and me as a baby." —Dan

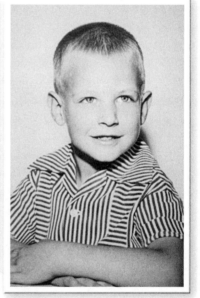

Dan, age 6 or 7

lessons to Dan. Her schedule at Dixie wouldn't allow her to provide the volume of sessions she instinctively knew he would want, and besides, she was always around to oversee while he practiced. In fact, she was often able to discern his mistakes even while tending to other issues in the house.

Dan, 10 years old

Christmas 1965. "My sister Rhonda and me. I've got my new Daniel Boone coonskin hat and rifle." —Dan

"When she was in the kitchen—and I remember this a lot—she would be, 'Nope, nope, nope, that's not right. That's not right. The fingering's wrong. Do something different,'" Dan laughs. "It was an educated guess,

"Mom at the piano. She can lay down the heavy stuff . . . Chopin, Bach, Rachmoninov."
—Dan

but she was usually right. Every so often, she'd come in and hang out for about five minutes when I was workin' on a piece. When I was working on a serious competition piece, she'd hang out even more, 'cause she had all these little drills and she knew all the tricks. She said, 'You can practice, but you're gonna get better if you practice right.' No matter what you're doin', if you use the right kind of techniques, you're gonna get there faster."

By the time Dan was eleven, he'd already soaked up most of the piano knowledge he could in a town of ten thousand people. He needed better instruction, a more worldly setting, and Karol started looking around Las Vegas for someone who could push her son further.

She found a German immigrant who'd moved to the United States in the 1950s, after World War II. Even though Vegas was a two-hour drive from St. George, the Trumans took Dan for regular visits to run through his drills and learn more advanced techniques at the foot of a master. The guy knew what he was doing, but he was a harsh, imposing figure— especially to a kid who was just entering his sensitive teen years.

1968. "How 'bout that family . . . and when are those hairstyles for women going to come back in?" —Dan

"He scared me to death," Dan recalls. "He still had a strong, strong accent, and I thought he was gonna pull out the little ruler and start hit-tin' me. He'd get mad at me, 'cause he could tell I hadn't practiced certain songs like I should. But it was a great experience, and probably the coolest thing now, lookin' back on it. I didn't understand this when my mom first told me this—but he lived right in Berlin in the '30s and '40s, and he taught all the big guys in the Third Reich, including Hitler's nieces and nephews. Now that I understand what that all means, I understand why he was so intense. And that brogue didn't help. He was already intense, but you add that German accent, wow!"

When the furor of the instructor's personality overtook the actual benefits of his instruction, Karol discontinued those lessons and had Dan study once again in the St. George area. A woman with a jazz background had moved to southwest Utah, and she kept him working on scales and phrasing and fingering techniques for another eighteen months.

The next section of his schooling, however, had all the hallmarks of a bad coming-of-age movie, a sort of *Risky Business* that's almost beyond believability. Karol found, yet again, a teacher who could take Dan's playing to the next level. Like the German terror, this new instructor—Marty Heim—was in Las Vegas.

Unlike the German, Mr. Heim was completely immersed in Vegas show business. He had a regular job playing five nights a week with his own trio at the island-themed Don the Beachcomber lounge in the Sahara Hotel. Mr. Heim had worked with Eartha Kitt and played Tony Bennett parties, and he took a respite from his lounge act to become Phyllis Diller's music director whenever the comedienne played the Strip.

Mr. Heim housed a huge amount of knowledge about the music business, and he was centered in a city with neon lights, gambling, and legal prostitution. Into that setting, the Trumans allowed their seventeen-year-old son to drive—*alone*—every other weekend for Friday afternoon lessons. They even let him stay overnight when he wanted—which was most of the time—because he had a friend he could stay with. Their only caveat: "Just be back Saturday afternoon." Not too many parents would give their teenage son that much leeway.

"The potential for disaster," Dan observes, "was high."

Dan and his buddy flirted with it too. They'd drive around Fremont Street, the original heart of wild and wooly Glitter Gulch, meet girls, and stay out into the early morning hours. Yet he managed to avoid trouble. His parents weren't afraid of it. They'd shown a huge amount of trust in Dan, and he wasn't about to blow it.

"That's probably why they did it," he says, though he'd already discovered that some aspects of life in the fast lane made it a not-so-appealing route.

"I used to work in this restaurant, playin' piano bar in St. George," Dan recalls. "One night at a party at that same hotel/restaurant where I was playing—the only thing I ever drank—I tried a beer and a rum. Growing up, there was not a whole lot of that around. When I tried it, I was like, *That beer sucks, man.* And the rum? Whoa.

"I was just never motivated to do it again, which is good because, boy, I saw a lot—particularly when I was playing clubs in the pre–Tennessee River Boys days—I saw a lot of musicians go through some tough times, you know, 'cause playin' clubs, usually the liquor was free for the band."

One particular story illustrates the comparative innocence with which Dan and his friends managed to navigate Sin City. He took a friend along to Vegas one Friday when he intended to drive back that night. They got to the Gulch around three o'clock, leaving Dan one hour to get to his lesson.

"I told him I'd pick him up at eleven o'clock," Dan remembers. "He said, 'I'll show you where I'll be'—'cause we didn't have cell phones then. He said, 'I'll be right here.' By a slot machine. They had penny slots.

"Sure enough, I pull up at eleven o'clock, eight hours later. I said, 'Whaddya been doin'?' He said, 'I've been right here playin' this slot. I grabbed a burger, but that took about five minutes.' He hadn't moved off that penny slot machine for eight hours. He said, 'I'm up $1.32!' I'll never forget; he was excited because he was up."

One of the famous lines from the Paul Anka–penned "My Way"— "Regrets . . . I've had a few"—somehow fits that period. For three years Dan traveled from St. George to Vegas every other Friday, and he saw some of the biggest names in twentieth-century entertainment on those marquees. And two of the guys who recorded "My Way"—Frank Sinatra and Elvis Presley—were accessible. Dan never took advantage of the opportunity.

"I should've seen Elvis," he says, "and I should've gone and seen the Rat Pack."

Delmont and Karol trusted Dan, but they were shocked when he announced his intention to work as a professional musician. They'd envisioned him in a more stable environment—music education, perhaps. The Trumans had seen firsthand the pitfalls of rock and pop music. A family acquaintance had gotten involved in a band and started experimenting heavily with drugs. He eventually died during a heroin trip.

Delmont's family experiences with damaged hands had led him to take a cautious role in guiding his son over something as nonthreatening as a school ring. This music thing—this was even more perilous, and the family experience suggested Dan could lose more than a finger; he might lose his life.

"That was the worst time for drugs in our culture," Dan says. "That's our most creative time, as far as music. Some of the best music obviously came out of the '70s, some of the best acts, but the drug thing was rampant."

Jimi Hendrix, Janis Joplin, Jim Morrison, Gram Parsons, Tim Buckley, Badfinger's Pete Ham, T. Rex's Tommy Bolin—the suicides and drug-related music deaths of that era were often highly publicized, and likewise romanticized. The accidental deaths of Chicago's Terry Kath and Elvis would only add to the issue.

"I can tell you horror stories—more than just that guy dying from heroin," Dan says. "I had another buddy that became an addict, another buddy that alcohol destroyed his life. I had another buddy that just got swallowed up in the L.A. thing so bad he destroyed everything—lost his wife, lost his career—and so that stuff was going on and always has gone on, and my folks were worried. But I remember standing outside of our church in St. George, Utah, my dad trying to talk me out of playing in bands, you know. I was eighteen years old."

"Me at 17. *What was I thinking?*" —Dan

The kid had managed to keep his nose clean on all those trips to Vegas. Delmont ultimately didn't have much choice; he needed to let Dan choose his own path. Delmont consented and may have been surprised when Dan began his adult life. First on Dan's agenda: a two-year mission trip to Florida on behalf of his church. He certainly had a commendable intent. And he followed it through. It wasn't as if he needed help to keep on the straight and narrow, but he received a poignant reminder of just how tenuous a life can be. One of the most moving duties he had during that stint came when he was asked to sing a duet during a memorial service at the end of a pier where a man was last seen before he drowned.

"I'm not really a good singer," Dan says. "I can carry a tune enough to be in a choir. But [that] was my most favorite performance."

After Florida, Dan headed back to school. He considered the prestigious Berklee School of Music in Boston but ultimately chose Brigham Young University, closer to home and extremely proficient in the arts. BYU maintained three jazz bands, and Dan played piano in the top

"My folks and me in 1975, right before I left for my two-year mission." —Dan

band, Synthesis. The group's concerts at the thirty-eight-hundred-seat de Jong Concert Hall routinely sold out.

Dan taught piano lessons on the side, at one point building a client base of twelve students, eleven of whom were referred to him by one of the BYU professors. And he took part in the BYU Young Ambassadors, a traveling entertainment group that represented the university around the U.S. and even on trips overseas.

1978. "One of my favorite bands, FANTASY. Scott Parker and Jeff Simper are still two of my dearest friends today." —Dan

The first of Dan's foreign treks with the Young Ambassadors was a trip to the Soviet Union that had a serendipitous result the Ambassadors referred to as the "Miracle of Montana." The troupe did a series of warm-up dates in Wyoming, Idaho, and Montana to prepare for a four-week visit to the Soviet Union in June 1978, followed by another week in Poland.

One of the employees at a small American TV station asked the group if, during its stay in Moscow, it could take a gift to a friend she knew. The BYU director obliged her and found out, only after setting up the appointment, that the Soviet woman was a huge television star, the Russian equivalent of Oprah Winfrey. She invited the Young Ambassadors to perform on her show, and—since the government ran just two stations for the entire country—the BYU students represented America behind the Iron Curtain to an audience of 150 million people. The episode ran numerous times, including in 1988 when improved relations between President Ronald Reagan and Soviet leader Mikhail Gorbachev created an interest in the U.S.S.R. for all things American.

Photograph by Mark A. Philbrick

"The Young Ambassadors in Russia in 1978. This picture is in Red Square in Moscow." —Dan

One unexpected development of the trip for Dan was more personal. He met a fellow Young Ambassador, Wendee Jensen. They got to know each other quickly and were soon a couple.

"We had five weeks there," Dan says. "We stood in a lot of bread lines together."

The couple married November 7, 1980, while still attending BYU. The schedule was crazy. Their studies, their work in the Young Ambassadors, his incessant practicing, the commitment to Synthesis, and the extra-curricular piano lessons he was giving all kept them separated for large chunks of each day.

The Young Ambassadors went abroad every year, and Dan and Wendee both participated in a 1982 trip to India, during which they sang "I Am a Child of God" in the Taj Mahal. The Ambassadors also gave a private performance for Indira Gandhi in the gardens at the palace, where the prime minister would be assassinated two years later. The trip was an eye-opening immersion into a culture that was radically different from anything the students knew.

"I've probably been in twenty-something different countries, but India is in a category of its own," Dan observes.

During the first half of the Young Ambassadors' trip, the students lived in homes with Indian families and quickly had to adjust to the native diet, which used exotic spices and did not include beef. Run-of-the-mill Indian food was frequently less palatable than the top-drawer versions of the country's cuisine that are served in the U.S.

"They had this ice cream—it's the most horrible in the world," Dan says. "To me, the meals were horrible [at the start]. And yet, after six weeks of bein' there, there was a lot of Indian food that I now love. I learned a great lesson there. You can learn to like stuff, and then learn to *really* like it, out of necessity."

During the latter portion of the trip, they stayed in Oberoi hotels, including the Oberoi Trident in Mumbai, where thirty-two people were killed during a 2008 attack by Pakistani terrorists.

From the time Dan left high school, it took a full decade to complete college. He'd spent two years in Florida before he started classes, and he withdrew periodically to hit the road with a couple of different bands. One of them—SunShade 'n' Rain—featured three vocalists in a big production that worked club dates, dinner theaters, and casino showrooms in Las Vegas and Reno.

"It was a white man's version of Earth, Wind & Fire," Dan says. "They always had a girl on stage. They were singin' 'You're the One That I Want' from *Grease,* or they would sing some Elvis tune, and that always would work. No matter what girl got on stage, when they'd sing one of those two songs, it translated big-time to that audience."

One of the singers also had a showy piano-and-vocal piece in the set that featured Dan as the only backup musician during a go-for-the-throat emotional moment.

"Literally he was so dramatic that he would be on his knees on 'Send in the Clowns,'" Dan remembers. "The audience would go crazy. I used to think all somebody has to do is see these guys and they'd sign their recording deal. What they would do to a crowd was just amazing. It never did happen."

The group often stayed in one place for a week or so at a stretch, and Dan made use of the time to hone his skills for the future. He might not be in a practice room at BYU, but he could certainly create one of his own at the club.

"Everybody thought I was crazy," he reflects, "but I really bought into this thing—and I was right—about 'I'm not as good a piano player as those piano players in L.A. and Nashville.' And so when I was on the road in those clubs, we usually had three sets a night in most of those clubs, so we were usually playin' from nine until one in the morning. But usually by eleven o'clock in the morning—sometimes earlier—I was back over there. I used to have the old electric grand. If it wasn't turned on, I could hear it, 'cause it had real strings, but it wasn't amplified.

"So even if there was a bar in the club, I could shut the curtain and I could practice; and it was my goal to practice at least four hours a day. Sometimes I'd get five or six hours in. Those were big-time, great years for me when I was on the road, because I wouldn't sleep in real late, I wouldn't go hang out real late. I wouldn't do it. I would practice."

Working for an Earth, Wind & Fire–style band, Dan had obviously not fallen into the trap that awaits many musicians trained in classical and/or jazz. He had no snobbery against popular music and, in fact, tended to embrace all of its forms. St. George had only a handful of radio stations, and the pop outlet had played everything from the Beatles to Mantovani when he was growing up. So Dan was familiar with a wide range of artists.

Johnny Cash and Merle Haggard had both made appearances on the station, and while country was built primarily around guitar, the textures that keyboard player John Probst brought to John Conlee's 1978 debut "Rose Colored Glasses" intrigued Dan. By the time Alabama had "Mountain Music" in circulation in country music in '82, Dan was playing keyboards for Synthesis, and he incorporated that song into the band's concerts, saving its closing solo section for himself.

The chords were much less complicated than jazz voicings, and Dan started taking out the middle note in country triads—the note that determines whether the chord is in a major or minor key— sometimes adding in a fourth. His chords were thus more spare, but allowed instrumental soloists—and, in vocal settings, the harmony singers—more flexibility.

"I would literally say to people—especially these jazz guys—'Don't get an attitude about country,'" Dan says. "Let it go. Enjoy everything."

Greatly influenced by Dan's diversity, the band director programmed one of the BYU concerts with an unusual mix of contemporary stuff. The show jumped from an Al Jarreau jazz song to Toto's pop signature

"Rosanna" to a crazy hybrid of a Loretta Lynn country classic that Dan and the Synthesis bass player had worked up.

"We had the horns step back and then just the rhythm section played," Dan says. "What I did was take the chord changes to 'Coal Miner's Daughter' and wrote a new melody, and the lyric was 'I'm just a jazz-playin' be-boppin' cowboy.' 'Be-Boppin' Cowboy' was the title of the song. Our bass player wrote that with me and sang it, and then me and the guitar player soloed over the country deal and then went into this jazz thing and came back into the country song. They went nuts in that audience."

Dan majored in music and minored in sociological statistics. He combined his interests by studying the national music charts to establish the kinds of songs that worked in different formats.

"One of my most enjoyable projects was just simply comparing with numbers what people listened to by reading the charts—what kind of subject matter people were listening to in pop music compared to the country chart," he recalls. "That was a fun one. It was a lot more songs about drugs on the pop charts, and there was a lot more songs that you didn't have any idea what they were talkin' about on the pop charts. And there was a lot more songs about—even in the '80s—a lot more songs about trains and dogs and mama on the country charts."

With the Young Ambassadors building a sense of showmanship in the school's music department, BYU became an annual audition site for Nashville's Opryland theme park, which needed young players to fill out the myriad productions on its amusement grounds. In 1982, the park hired Wendee. Dan took classes for a couple of months, then visited Tennessee for about ten days near the end of summer.

Both of them liked Nashville, and Wendee chatted up Dan's abilities with Lloyd Wells, Opryland's musical director, in hopes of landing a job for her husband the next year. Dan had traveled the U.S. with a club band, he'd performed around the world, he was the band director for the

Young Ambassadors, and he knew a ton of styles. He was, it seemed, a perfect guy for the park.

When Dan auditioned for the 1983 season, Lloyd asked him to stick around and play piano for several other tryouts. It gave him an opportunity to see how Dan would handle performing on the fly. He got the job in the blue cast for *Country Music USA*.

Dan adapted quickly to Nashville, though the couple returned to Utah when the park's season was over. They were rehired the next year, but stuck around Utah long enough for their first son, Ben, to arrive June 2. Two weeks later they once again headed in their rickety Volkswagen Rabbit to Nashville.

At his father's urging, Dan had protected his hands and practiced diligently to make them a part of the career he had in mind. The Tennessee River Boys—yet another ensemble at Opryland—would play a huge part in that career, though Dan didn't realize at the time that the breakthrough would take a difficult six years to arrive.

chapter 5

JIMMY OLANDER

Russ Harrington

*M*usic in Detroit took some weird turns right around 1974. Motown, the label that practically defined the city for a decade, left the Motor City in 1972, leaving a void in its core identity. Ted Nugent, a gonzo hard-rocker, played slash-and-burn with the Amboy Dukes for one last album before launching a solo career. Bob Seger established his blue-collar Silver Bullet Band. And some adults—perhaps spurred by a fondness for Roy Clark on *Hee Haw*—found themselves taking banjo lessons from a twelve-year-old kid.

That kid, Jimmy Olander, was something of a prodigy, a guy who built quite a bank account by amassing fees from students before he ever figured out exactly what he should do with his life. Little did he know that what he was doing there at Music, Strings & Things was actually forming the foundation for his eventual vocation.

Though he began developing his musical identity in Michigan, Jimmy established a competitive spirit out West as his parents, Bill and the former Margie Beirman, moved around. Jimmy was born August 26, 1961, in Minneapolis, but his dad wasn't particularly happy in Minnesota, and a year later the family moved to California.

"I love my older brother Doug." —Jimmy

Doug (5 yrs.) Jimmy (3 yrs.) "I love my mom, too, but she's gonna pay for dressing us in those sweaters . . . *Mom!*" —Jimmy

The family lived for about five years in Palos Verdes, a coastal community south of the Los Angeles airport, where Jimmy started driving quarter-midget race cars when he was five years old. The Olanders spent another five years in Fremont, between San Jose and Oakland at the southeast edge of San Francisco Bay. During that time Jimmy won the state quarter-midget championship. It was a family endeavor. Jimmy's older brother, Doug, raced as well; Margie was a timekeeper; and Bill looked constantly for ways to modify the cars and give the kids an edge.

"He did these kooky things," Jimmy recalls. "Like he had come up with his own compound of rubber that would cure at track temperature.

"Five years old with a need for speed. I was nicknamed 'Lightning' ironically because I was so slow my first year racing." —Jimmy

It would get sticky, and the tires would get better traction. So the entire time we were living in Fremont in quarter-midget racing, we had these huge freezers out in the garage and the freezer in the house and you opened it up, there weren't any frozen waffles in there. There were quarter-midget tires."

They soon added sailboat racing to the family's activities. The sport required the racer to pilot a dinghy with his feet on a small rod above the water, which left eight-year-old Jimmy on his own over the deep waters of the San Francisco Bay, attempting to beat the competition to the finish line.

Again, Bill looked for an advantage. Margie sewed together four sweatshirts to add bulk to their lightweight boy, and Bill would dunk him in the water to add a good forty to fifty pounds and give Jimmy more control of his craft. That left Jimmy out on the water, his teeth chattering against the stiff San Francisco winds.

"You couldn't modify these boats at all, but you could paint them," Jimmy says, "so he always found a way to bend the rules—it wasn't illegal, but he painted all the bottoms of his boats with a liquid graphite and would wet-sand these things. We'd paint the bottom of these boats with graphite, and it was slicker than snot, and we'd go like a bat out of hell."

Something about his father's side of the family was particularly harsh. Bill had little tolerance for incompetence. Grandfather Olander was downright un-grandfatherly, at least from a seven-year-old's perspective.

"My grandfather and I did not like each other," Jimmy recalls. "It's an odd thing to realize as a young kid and pass the judgment that, *You know what? He doesn't like me, and I've tried really hard.* You kinda come to grips with that, and it no longer hurts your feelings. At the time I decided: *You know what? Because of that, I don't like him either.*"

After Fremont, the Olanders headed back to the Midwest, settling in Birmingham, Michigan, just before Jimmy started the sixth grade. For a time it appeared Jimmy might not make the move. Bill relocated while the family sold the house, but Jimmy grew dangerously ill. The family doctor at first diagnosed him with a severe case of the flu, but when his temperature reached 107 degrees, Margie found another doctor who discovered Jimmy had spinal meningitis.

Jimmy went into convulsions and underwent an emergency spinal tap. Bill feared he might lose his son and tried to fly back. When he was unable to get a plane out, he enlisted a coworker to drive with him across country to be there for Jimmy, who ultimately survived, though he insists he did "fry some brain cells" during his illness.

He was still a smart kid, but he didn't always feel it. His brother was *really* smart, and Bill—well, Jimmy's dad really *was* a rocket scientist. He worked on the research team that helped GM build the catalytic converter. He took a job during the 1980s with the Department of Defense when Ronald Reagan introduced the Strategic Defense Initiative—otherwise known as the Star Wars defense system. Bill also consulted in the development of the LinnDrum, one of the first drum machines, influential in early-'80s pop by the likes of the Human League, Prince, Phil Collins, and the Thompson Twins.

His father's use of electronics—and his attempts to use science to improve his son's sports performance—helps explain how Jimmy, who started out on an acoustic instrument such as a banjo in a diehard acoustic genre like bluegrass, might ultimately end up using technology to advance his own unique sound.

Jimmy started on banjo mostly because it was what was available at the house. Back in Minnesota, his dad had taken lessons on a four-string tenor banjo, a Martin model built from mahogany. His dad's original teacher, Bill Peer, had drawn out some very intricate chord diagrams—much more detailed than the guitar tab instructions found in most sheet music. Jimmy figured out the system pretty quickly, and his dad promised that if he practiced and became really good on the instrument, he'd buy him a real five-string banjo.

"I was not necessarily a magnet for girls growing up. I don't know if it was the banjo or the corduroys with the exploded ink pen stain on my pocket." —Jimmy

Jimmy did his homework, got his new banjo, and took lessons for six months from Maggie Taylor at Music, Strings & Things, "this little hippy-dippy music store on Woodward Avenue." Between lessons he absorbed himself in transcribing banjo parts from vinyl records, picking up the needle and moving it back to hear certain passages repeatedly until he could grasp what the players were doing.

"Imagine the sponge of a twelve-year-old brain, studying banjo eight hours a day, playing constantly," Jimmy says. "Kids can pick up [things] really fast. I see that now that I'm an adult and can't remember anything. Kids, their development just goes *sssss-hoop*! I was right in that period."

After his six months with Maggie, Jimmy spent another six months of intense self-study on the instrument, then returned to Music, Strings & Things with a mixture of boldness and innocence to ask for a job as a banjo instructor for intermediate and advanced students.

"My dad had to kinda plead the case at the music store because I was twelve," Jimmy laughs. "The good news was that they not only did not wanna be racist, I remember the term 'ageist': 'We're not ageist either.'"

The job paid good money for a junior high student. Jimmy earned $5.50 per half hour of instruction and often had thirty to forty students per week. That's roughly $165 or more in weekly income and no bills for food, rent, or utilities. Jimmy, in fact, saved up enough to buy a 1953 GMC pickup and restored it when he was fifteen years old— again a bit precocious, since he couldn't drive it on his own until his sixteenth birthday.

"Ageism" might not have been appropriate in music instruction or in the purchase of a vehicle, but it was a ground rule at clubs. Dad was quite supportive of Jimmy's musical interests, so he accompanied the boy on occasion to music shows. The Raven Gallery, a non-alcoholic location on Woodward, featured

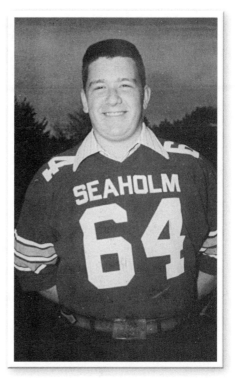

High school sophomore. Tackle. "I can still remember seeing this picture for the first time and thinking, *Hey I'm looking kinda slim.* It really is all about perspective, isn't it?" —Jimmy

one show that would prove significant in Jimmy's future: he saw IInd Generation, a bluegrass act led by banjo player Eddie Adcock; the mandolin player, Gene Johnson, was destined to become a bandmate.

Once Jimmy could actually drive, he started playing in the region with Lawrence Lane & the Kentucky Grass, a bluegrass act that recorded for Rome Records. Jimmy also ordered a custom-made gold-plated banjo from Gruhn Guitars in Nashville and drove down to Music City to pick it up when it was completed.

"As I'm coming out of Louisville, I saw those big green signs on the interstate, goin' to Nashville," Jimmy remembers. "I thought, *Wouldn't it be great if one day I could ride a tour bus?* That's how small my dreams were."

Lawrence Lane and Kentucky Grass—Marion, Ohio. *Left to right:* Jim Greer, Mary Lane, Jimmy O, Chris Kolms, Jeff Whitaker; seated, Lawrence Lane. "By this time as a banjo player [age 16] I had finally made it to the next level. In bluegrass we refer to this as the 'Matching Shirts and Matching Hats Level.' Very exclusive." —Jimmy

That idea seemed rather remote. The Olander boys had been raised under the assumption that they would attend college. And that was not, as best as anyone knew, a direct route to life on a tour bus.

"This wasn't 'What do you wanna do? Are you gonna go get a factory job or somethin'?' No," Jimmy says. "Both of my parents were graduates of the University of Minnesota. We were college people. My brother went to college after graduation. I was going to college—I mean it was not even an option."

Having devoted his attention to the banjo and the guitar and teaching students, Jimmy had posted rather pedestrian grades. His brother might be qualified to attend a prestigious school such as Stanford, but Jimmy needed to think about something more reasonable. Restaurant management at Michigan State looked like a logical choice, until one day Bill came home from work with news about some Tennessee school called Belmont. It had a music business school with a recording studio on campus, and it was literally blocks from Music Row, where all of Nashville's major record labels ran their operations.

It didn't take a rocket scientist—even if Jimmy's dad was one—to figure out that Belmont was a good option. And Jimmy didn't wait. The same week he graduated from high school in 1979, he packed his possessions into the bed of his '53 pickup, drained his bank account, and headed back down the interstate, under the green signs that pointed to Nashville, to find his fortune.

"'Old Red.' I loved that truck. It suffered its demise at the wheels of a speeding Fiat on Belmont Blvd., Nashville. May it RIP." —Jimmy

"I moved to Nashville with no intention of going back home," he says. "I love my folks. I went back and visited on holidays and stuff like that, but summertime, I worked in Nashville."

Plenty of artists have since used Belmont as a stepping-stone to find their way into the music business. Ty Herndon, Brad Paisley, Lee Ann Womack, Trisha Yearwood, Josh Turner, Restless Heart's Larry Stewart—they're just a few of the acts who figured out they could balance collegiate aims with their musical passions at the school off Wedgewood Avenue.

Jimmy was one of the first to figure that out. He also figured out that he could make money as a rhythm guitar player at Opryland, and he got a job in the blue cast of *Country Music USA*, which used costume changes and vocal impressions to give park-goers a capsule summary of country's history.

One of the fringe benefits, though it wasn't necessarily approved by park officials, was a chance to see the Grand Ole Opry's Tuesday matinees and to attend sometimes on Friday and Saturday nights when someone he knew had access.

"I had friends that played for artists on the Opry," Jimmy says. "That was all part of a deal where [I started thinking], *Man, I could actually play for one of these acts? Maybe Bill Anderson?* I remember goin' back and seein' Bill Anderson . . . Bill actually had production. He set up on a Tuesday matinee, and he had video screens and he had electronic drum sounds and he had backup singers and they all had matchin' outfits, and I was like, *Wow, that must be the coolest gig I've ever seen in my life!*"

That dream of traveling on a tour bus was starting to look as if it were in reach. Jimmy was getting to spend some time in the company of the stars. He wasn't just seeing his friends work with Opry stars; he was hanging out with one of the biggest, Roy Acuff, at *Country Music USA.*

"It was like the only season that [the show] was in the Acuff Theater," Jimmy says. "It was a summertime gig, everybody was sweatin' their [butts] off in these polyester outfits, and I was in the Acuff in the air-conditioning all day long. Roy would come from his house and go to the Roy Acuff Theater, and he'd come back and sit with the band—because we had perfect vantage of the girls dressing as they did their costume changes. And he loved it.

"He did it so much that they made Roy a part of the show, and the climax of the show was a guy would come out and sing 'I'm So Lonesome I Could Cry' in a Hank Williams Sr. outfit. When Roy would come and sit down and watch that stuff, they'd give him the jacket and he'd go out and finish the show. He was such a kooky old guy, but a cute old guy."

Given the inroads he was making off campus, Jimmy decided to quit Belmont and go at the music business from a different angle.

"I wasn't learning a lot, and I was paying my way through college," he

© 2009 Grand Ole Opry Archives

Roy Acuff

explains. "It was very expensive, and whatever fortune I moved to Nashville with I was spending, so I dropped out of college."

His specialty instrument, the banjo, was a bit limited, particularly in the *Urban Cowboy* era. Within a year of Jimmy's arrival, the John Travolta movie—combined with the cultural impact of the Larry Hagman nighttime soap *Dallas*—had created a huge interest in country music and Western fashion. Willie Nelson, Anne Murray, Waylon Jennings, Charlie Daniels, Don Williams, Mickey Gilley, Johnny Lee, Ronnie Milsap, Eddie Rabbitt, Crystal Gayle—they all had crossover hits, most of them slick. And none of them used banjo.

Jimmy could play acoustic guitar chords, but he was worthless as a lead player, and he knew he needed some chops on electric guitar if he was going to get a job as a studio musician or in the road band for a major star. He went on a six-month crash course learning to play guitar, again applying his transcription abilities to learn the instrument.

"I would transcribe the country Top 20 off of the radio," he says. "This is back in the days of cassette tapes, where the receiver and the cassette tape were in the same machine, so when a song came on, I'd push Record and then I'd learn all the guitar licks for that. I couldn't play guitar and sit in and jam with people, but if you wanted me to play the licks—the exact licks that were on the record—I could regurgitate this stuff. I didn't know *what* I was playing, but I could sound like them."

In the process, Jimmy ended up a long way from where he'd begun his musical journey. He'd started as a banjo player in bluegrass music, where electric instruments were frowned upon. He'd studied Earl Scruggs, developed a taste for newgrass, a progressive brand of bluegrass, and discovered through that a connection to jazz. He'd started playing his banjo on top of jazz records, which led him to swing, where he discovered Leon Rhodes, the lead guitar player for Ernest Tubb's Texas Troubadours. That had opened Jimmy up to all the contemporary country hits, and he had become a regular customer at the Great Escape, a used record store on Broadway, where he picked up as many albums as he could afford—the good and the bad—to learn this new genre.

At the same time, Mel Deal—the steel player in *Country Music USA*—was friends with Joe Glaser, a guitar-maker who'd recently moved to Nashville from northern California. Clarence White, who'd played guitar with the Byrds, had developed something called a "bender," a device that allowed a guitarist to raise the pitch on a string as much as a full note by activating a gizmo attached to the guitar strap. It allowed a player to approach his instrument like a steel guitar and tweak notes or entire passages without creating any extra finger work.

Building on that advancement, Joe had invented a new double-bender guitar with a latch that hooked on to the guitar player's belt. By pulling the guitar away from the body, the latch tightened the string and raised the note, and the double-bender actually worked on *two* different strings.

Jimmy had a thing for the sound of steel guitar, even though he didn't know how to play it, but with the double-bender, he could now transcribe steel guitar parts for an electric guitar and somehow make them work. He was using banjo finger techniques, steel phrasing, and a new guitar effect, and since he was just learning the instrument for the first time, it all became a natural part of his sound.

Terry Wendt, a steel guitarist he met at Belmont, convinced Jimmy to join a regional bar band, Smooth Sailing, and they toured the club circuit, scratching out a bottom-rung subsistence with little pay and junk food.

"You get a hotel room or a band room," Jimmy says, "you're living on fish heads and rice and pickles every week, whatever is cheap that has volume."

Surprisingly, the brainy Olander family was completely supportive: "Whatever you want to do," they told him.

Left to right: Duane Burnash, Jimmy Olander, Terry Wendt (kneeling), and Bobby Green. Smooth Sailing, '81 or '82. "Did I really drop out of college for this?" —Jimmy

Bobby Green, one of his bandmates in Smooth Sailing, had already crossed paths with Jimmy. His sister, Barbara, had been one of the vocalists in *Country Music USA*.

"She was pretty, and she was a full-on great country singer," Jimmy says.

Bobby worked clubs around Nashville a lot when Smooth Sailing wasn't on tour, and whenever a date came up, he inevitably called Jimmy.

"I don't sing at all, [so] there was a lot of charity that had to be extended to me," Jimmy says. "I was probably a lot better guitar player than what was available to do those club gigs, but you know what? It really doesn't matter if I'm that much better than this guy, 'cause this guy can sing fifteen songs a night and we're gonna have to come up with forty. So to have me on the gig meant that somebody had to sing an extra fifteen songs, and Bobby always included me on his gigs. So I had a strong connection to that family."

Jimmy started dating another of Bobby's sisters, Belinda, though the relationship was doomed from the start. She was a lesbian in an era when few people in the South were willing to acknowledge it publicly. Everyone around him seemed to recognize it, but Jimmy was completely in the dark until he went to a party also attended by Belinda's girlfriend, who was harsh and belligerent toward Jimmy the entire night.

"I was blind as a box of rocks—it literally had to be thrown in my face for me to get this," Jimmy laughs. "It's like where you see in the movie where you go, *Does stuff like this really happen? Is somebody this stupid?* And they finally go, *Ooooooh.* It was comical. You can't write comedy like that."

All the pieces suddenly fit, and in the shock of it all, Jimmy ended up with Barb, the former *Country Music USA* singer.

"I looked at Barb and said, 'What are you doin'? Let's get out of here.' She was broken up with her old man, and that was it. All of a sudden we were married."

In 1981, Mel McDaniel, a scratchy-voiced Oklahoman who was just catching his stride with Capitol Records, enlisted Jimmy to play guitar, and that certainly fulfilled his previous dream of riding a tour bus. He grew comfortable on the road with Mel, and the musical part of the gig was fairly easy since Mel mostly wanted Jimmy to imitate the parts some other guitarist had already worked out on the recorded versions of his songs. Meanwhile, Jimmy continued practicing his double-bender guitar, and his proficiency was improving.

He also played a lot of Nashville club dates, doing his best imitations of the established session musicians—such as Phil Baugh, Brent Rowan, and Reggie Young—who were leaving their marks on the hits of the time by George Jones, John Conlee, Hank Williams Jr., and the Oak Ridge Boys. Joe Glaser, the double-bender manufacturer, had a band that played out regularly, and Jimmy sat in with the group frequently. Joe wasn't shy about steering him in new directions.

"He's watching my development as a guitar player, and he's also having serious discussions with me about style and voice," Jimmy recalls. "He'd say, 'Man, you're really playing this guy's lick really well. That's awesome.'"

But Joe also pointed out that Phil Baugh, Brent Rowan, and Reggie Young were already being paid good money to do their own licks. It was a signature, and the imitators weren't making a name for themselves: "You need to really work on what you're going to do."

Jimmy wanted to be one of those guys and quit the job with Mel McDaniel to focus his energies on playing in Nashville. With less of his time chewed up by bus travel, he had more time to practice. He also had more time to see what a mess he was in with Barbara, who wasn't working. Without the pay from Mel, they were making less than $8,000 a year. Suddenly, the kid who'd cleared $165 a week as a teenager in Detroit needed financial help from his dad.

"He was like, 'You need a car? Let me buy you a car,'" Jimmy says. "He was never able to do that for me in high school, and I never really realized that being self-sufficient [deprived my parents]. I always thought that they were whispering, 'Pay your own way through college' while I was sleeping, but actually one of the benefits of being a parent is to provide for your kids, and I took a little bit of that away from them."

Jimmy's financial desperation in the '80s gave his parents that opportunity.

"Luckily"—he winks—"I became a little bit of a musician low-life, and they helped me out."

It was okay for a short period, but Jimmy was determined to make his own money—even if it meant he had to take a job that wasn't quite at the level he'd reached. It would only be temporary. The boy from the Motor City was going to make it in Music City one way or another. He just didn't know yet that the answer was back at Opryland.

chapter 6

BRIAN PROUT

Russ Harrington

*B*rian Prout identifies strongly with the George Bailey character in the classic movie *It's a Wonderful Life*. George grew up with huge ambitions in Bedford Falls, a fictitious small town in upstate New York where he had his ears slapped back by an employer and watched his father fight against forces that beat him down.

Brian was likewise born in upstate New York—in Troy, on December 4, 1955—and watched his father struggle against bigger forces. In this case, it was Brian's dad, Charles, who handed out the physical punishment to the kid. And while Charles might have had his Mr. Potters to battle, his biggest enemy was his own mind. The elder Prout never did have the Christmas Eve epiphany that led him to discover it really was a wonderful life. One other big difference separated Brian from George Bailey. Brian got out of Troy and eventually lived out the vocational dream he'd envisioned growing up.

Troy, New York, Brian around age 6 months

Beyond *It's a Wonderful Life*, the picture *Field of Dreams* resonates often in Brian's mind, primarily because of the end-of-the-movie image when Kevin Costner sees his father step out from an Iowa cornfield and offer to play catch with him. Kevin's character suddenly has a chance to see his dad before the world beat him up, an opportunity Brian wished he could have had.

In fact, the full details of his father's torment were never clear to Brian until after Diamond Rio committed to this biography. Three months after the birth of his oldest son, Delbert, Charles was called to service during World War II, and he served under Gen. Joseph Stilwell, building the Burma Road, a supply route in India.

The Allies faced a disaster in Burma (now Myanmar), which was captured for a time by the Japanese. Numerous Americans lost their lives, and Charles was nearly one of them. He had a bayonet thrust into his back during hand-to-hand combat. He choked his assailant to death—hearing the soldier's final wheeze and feeling his body go limp in his hands—with the knife still protruding from between his shoulder blades.

"My dad's official army portrait." —Brian

circa 1942–1944. "My dad serving in the Burmese jungle during WW II." —Brian

Charles won a Purple Heart for his actions, but after healing he was thrust back into the conflict. By the time he returned to New York, Delbert was three years old and Charles was no longer the man Leah Prout had married. Throughout the rest of his life, the wound would occasionally fester, and Leah was left to squeeze the pus out—and to deal with Charles's anger.

The men of that time period didn't talk about feelings, and Charles was certainly a man of his era. He spoke to Leah only once of his experiences on the battlefield, demanding that the topic never be addressed again. He struggled with the demons on his own, frequently using alcohol to numb his emotions.

The Prouts had a daughter, Flora, two years after the war's end. Brian came along in 1955, and another daughter, Lori, followed two years later.

"I'm convinced that I was an 'oops' and my younger sister was an 'oh no, not again!'" Brian laughs.

The five Prouts—Del had already moved out—occupied twelve hundred square feet at 142 McChesney Avenue, east of Troy, where Brian learned to golf in a nearby cow pasture during the summer and learned to ski on an adjacent hill during the winter.

Charles owned a slaughterhouse—not a mass-production, hundreds-of-cattle-a-day plant; a small operation where one cow, maybe two, was killed each day, cut up, and distributed to local grocers. Brian was put to work by the time he was five or six.

"The cattle trucks would show up," Brian remembers. "The cattle would come down the chute, Dad put the gun between the slats, popped 'em in the head, they'd drop, wrap a chain around the ankles, raise it up."

Charles would carve the animal up for redistribution. Brian helped clean up the mess, and he was expected to use common sense, even at age six or seven.

"My mom [wore] my [butt] out with a yardstick," he says, "because I'd ruined a brand-new pair of Keds sneakers sweepin' blood into the drain after a fresh kill in the slaughterhouse."

The job was drudgery, and Charles worked at it ten to fourteen hours a day. Brian figured out rather quickly that it was not the kind of work schedule he wanted to commit to as an adult, even if it did have its fringe benefits.

"Nobody wants to see how it's made," Brian explains, "but I still haven't found anybody who makes as good a sausage as my father made."

When the business tapered off, Charles opened a mom-and-pop grocery store, still specializing in fresh meats. Suppliers brought the entire carcass to his shop and Charles did the butchery in the cooler—less of a mess, less stinky, but he still put in long, grueling hours every day.

Leah enrolled Brian in dance classes, as she'd done for Flora, and Brian had a natural talent for it— perhaps an early indicator of the

Troy, New York. "I was the Skyliners drum and bugle corps' mascot. In this picture I was 8 or 9 years old." —Brian

rhythm that would eventually propel him creatively. He was impressed by modern jazz, Fred Astaire, and Gene Kelly, and he kept dancing until he was seventeen, performing mostly with his younger sister, Lori. But dancing was the source of ridicule as he became a teen, and it slowly receded into the background in Brian's life.

His father was a leader in the Skyliners, a drum and bugle corps associated with the Troy Boys' Club. The group went out of town periodically to compete in contests, and Brian naturally landed in the corps.

"It was straight-up military, these wool outfits on one-hundred-degree days," Brian says. "You're marching down in a parade, and doin' these contests, and kids are droppin' like flies, passin' out from dehydration. But the discipline of the corps—you are a member of the corps. It's a sum of the parts. Nobody's the star. The corps is the star. And so I took that attitude from the drum and bugle corps, which my father insisted I be a part of. That's where I got my chops for playing—and the discipline and the rehearsals and everything that goes along with it."

"My younger sister Lori is on the right. This was an annual Flag Day parade in Troy, New York, home of the original 'Uncle Sam': Sam Wilson. The moms made sparkly vests to match the drums." —Brian

The music in the Prout household was primarily classical, jazz, and traditional pop—Tony Bennett remains a personal favorite more than forty years later—but the introduction of the Beatles on the *Ed Sullivan Show* inspired Brian, as it did millions of teenagers around America in 1964. Charles was less than impressed by the mop-top lads from Liverpool.

"Bring out the mouse!" he bellowed, referring to Topo Gigio, a silly puppet that was a semi-regular on *Sullivan.*

But Flora, who would finish first runner-up the following year in a Junior Miss pageant, had a different response, and it made an impression on her younger brother. Flora was crazy about the Beatles, and if someone who had it together as much as Flora could be moved by these guys playing rock 'n' roll, then Brian wanted to do that too.

He was already showing he had some talent as a drummer, and since he kept hammering away at the idea of being like Ringo Starr, Flora went down to Romeo's Music on Broadway, just a couple of blocks from the

"Flora bought me my first drum set in '64 or '65, when I was 8 or 9. This is Christmas morning. Lori is on the left with her keyboard." —Brian

Hudson River in downtown Troy, and bought Brian his first real drum kit for Christmas. The drums ended up a good outlet for Brian's energies. Girls liked musicians, and as he moved into his teen years, playing built some confidence. Plus, he was able to channel whatever anger he had into banging on the instrument, and there was plenty of hostility passed around the Prout household.

Charles, submerging his rage from Burma, used alcohol to battle the emotional pain.

"If he got into it too much, he had quite the belligerent side, to the point where Mom was yankin' us kids out of bed in the middle of the night and throwin' us in the car and flyin' out of there," Brian says. "'Dad's on a rampage!' And a couple of different times there were restraining orders placed on him, [so] he couldn't come around."

In one of the worst episodes, Charles threatened the family with a butcher's knife.

"My dad was not gonna slice our throats that night," Brian says. "He was just in his own little world, his own little rage, but my mother saw fit that night to take us out of that home, and rightfully so, because who knows how that would've ended up? He may have been having a flashback to his complication with that soldier."

Charles enrolled several times in detox programs but invariably left within a few days.

"I ask Mom to this day, 'Why did we stay with Dad? Why did *you* stay with Dad?'" Brian says. "[Even with] the restraining orders, he still would show up, and we'd have to call the police and all this other stuff. And yet Mom chose to stay. She says, 'He was my husband. It was a different time, it was a different generation, and 'til death do us part meant 'til death do us part. I recognized that alcoholism is a disease, but so is cancer, and I would not have left him if he had that.'"

Charles did his best. The family never went hungry. He worked long hours making ends meet, tried to instill some discipline, and supported

Brian's desire to play the drums. Not every parent would've allowed all that racket in the house.

Brian had to finish his homework before he could practice, and one particular day Leah had taken the girls shopping. Alone in the house with his dad, the boy was summoned.

"Brian!"

"Yes, sir?"

"Get down here!"

"I was fully expecting him to come around the corner and the belt come out—I assumed I'd forgotten to do something I was supposed to," Brian says. "I got down there, and on the kitchen table was a bottle of Miller High Life beer, a shot of bourbon, a pack of Chesterfield cigarettes, and a condom—sittin' right here. I'm sixteen years old, and I'm like, 'Yes, sir?' 'Oh, well, your mother said I need to talk to you about all this.' So I sat there at the kitchen table with my dad. We drank the beer, we drank the shot of bourbon and smoked a couple of those nasty Chesterfield cigarettes. But he wouldn't let me keep the condom."

Charles could tell Brian about the facts of life. But outside of the drum and bugle corps, Charles knew little about music. Fortunately, Brian had Ralph Purificato, a drum instructor who played weekend jazz gigs in nearby Albany.

Ralph was a large guy who kept a drum kit set up in the lower level of his house for lessons, and he knew the circuit in upstate New York well. You could earn thirty or forty dollars a night, and there was plenty of work to be had if you were willing to commute to other club gigs. Boston was a three-hour drive east on Interstate 90. Manhattan was 150 miles downstream along the Hudson. Lake George, a resort area north in the Adirondacks, had plenty of work opportunities. And the Catskills were only an hour away, though that resort area—once a bustling entertainment outpost that paid top dollar for Sammy Davis Jr., Red Buttons, and Danny Kaye—was well past its prime.

Ralph saw the handwriting on the wall for his type of music. He saw potential in Brian and also saw that schooling the boy in a dying art form such as traditional pop might prevent his student from truly excelling in the real world with rock 'n' roll clearly taking over. So Ralph discontinued the lessons.

"I learned more from Ralph probably away from the drums than I did on the drums," Brian reflects. "Eugene Kane, my band instructor in high school, was very similar. He said, 'Brian, I think you've got something. If you're goin' after it, treat it like a business. This is your job.'"

Mr. Kane underscored his belief in Brian during his senior year by presenting him the inaugural Roger Fulkerson Memorial Award, named for a drummer who graduated from Troy High School in 1965, only to lose his life in Vietnam. Years later, Brian had a copy of Diamond Rio's first double-platinum album made for Mr. Kane. When he shipped off the plaque, he included an imprint he'd made of Roger Fulkerson's name from the Vietnam Veterans Memorial in Washington DC.

$$\natural \,\clef{treble}\, \natural$$

While Leah did her best to keep the Prout household from coming unglued, the kids couldn't wait to leave. When Brian was three, Delbert had joined the marines at age seventeen and moved away. Flora was married by the time she was twenty.

Brian moved out within two weeks of his high school graduation in June 1974, though he stayed in the city. He picked up club gigs on the weekends and washed cars during the day. By chance one evening, he stopped on the way home at a bar where he ran into his older brother, Del, who hadn't bothered to mention he was staying in town for a night. Separated by fourteen years, they'd never really bonded, but Del started asking the kid about his life. *What are your goals? Where do you want to live? Mom and Dad say you're playing really good—why are you here in Troy?*

Brian was in a band, he had a girlfriend, and he was making a little coin, though not a lot.

Del put his arm around his little brother: "You have got to leave. If this is what you wanna do, it's not in Troy, New York."

Before they left the tavern, Del gave Brian a hundred-dollar bill and told him to put it in the bank and keep adding to it until he could afford to get out.

George Bailey had received an epiphany at a bar. And now Brian Prout had too.

"That night, and that man—my brother—changed the course of my life, hands down," Brian says. "Without that, I'd have been perfectly content to be the big fish in a small pond in upstate New York."

"Brian, Mom, and Del (my older brother) at Del's house in Greenbrier, Arkansas, 1994–95." —Brian

It took a few years. Brian's escape money grew slowly. As he built his bank account, he had yet another epiphany. A friend who worked week-ends on the local country station, WGNA-FM, got tickets for Brian and his girlfriend, Penny Knight, to see Emmylou Harris and Vassar Clements at the Palace Theatre in Albany. Emmylou's musicians, the Hot Band, were "stupid good," Brian says, and the following day Brian went out and bought a copy of her *Elite Hotel* album. It was the beginning of his transition into country music.

With his brother's admonition in mind, he looked into other places to live. His bandmates were all focused on getting married and starting families. He knew he'd have to leave alone and start over. New York was an obvious choice, but the city didn't suit him and it was close enough to home that it would be easy to give up. Instead, he set his sights on South Florida. It would be a make-it-or-break-it situation, and when his girlfriend—a fellow drummer—gave him the "I need my space" speech, it sealed the deal.

"I thought, *Well, okay, fifteen hundred miles oughta be enough space*," he laughs.

Summer of '82. Brian Prout, age 26.

Brian arrived in Fort Lauderdale in 1979, and with his New York background he was quickly drawn to the Galt Ocean Mile Hotel, the place at which Joe Namath had once guaranteed the upstart Jets would win a Super Bowl. The beach resort was the spring-training residence for the New York Yankees, and Brian wound up playing classics such as "I've Got You Under My Skin" in a jazz combo while the likes of Reggie Jackson, Thurman Munson, Bucky Dent, and Yankees owner George Steinbrenner told stories and impressed women. At night he freelanced for rock bands.

But the Galt job dried up in the summer, and Brian needed more steady work. So he popped into Cowboy's, a former discotheque that had transitioned—as did many clubs during the *Urban Cowboy* era—into a country dance hall. The owner was looking, as it happened, for a deejay to spin records, and Brian talked his way into the job, coming in early in the afternoons to learn the tempos and musical arc of the music.

Cowboy's was the home of the Hot Walker Band, an outlaw-flavored group that included guitarist Les Strader and his brother, drummer Arlen Strader. Arlen had decided to go back to school, and after he asked Brian to sit in one night, Brian became the band's permanent drummer. It was a prime slot, particularly because he got to watch a parade of major acts—Alabama, Mickey Gilley, Jerry Lee Lewis, Earl Thomas Conley, David Frizzell & Shelly West—work the crowd.

Fort Lauderdale—"Snort Liquordale," as he liked to call it—was uncomfortable for Brian. The Don Johnson TV series *Miami Vice*, destined to appear on TV sets a few years later, glamorized what could be a treacherous atmosphere—the sun, the shady characters, the busy nightlife, the cocaine. It wasn't how Brian intended to live out his days.

Driving home one Saturday morning in 1982 after staying out all night, he stopped his thirteen-year-old converted phone truck at a red light in front of a church he'd occasionally attended. While Brian's vehicle idled, the church's maintenance man finished putting a new message on the sign out front: "Would the Boy You Were Be Proud of the Man You Are?"

The answer was easy: no.

The message for the twenty-six-year-old drummer was simple: time to make a change.

"Everybody I was around and working with in bands and my social circles was in their mid- and early thirties, or their late thirties—some of 'em were even in their early forties—just tryin' to hang on to their youth and carrying on like they were on spring break year-round," Brian recalls. "I knew that wasn't for me."

Within a few weeks he got another message. His father had died

September 29. Brian had a funeral to attend in Troy. It wasn't just sad—it was disappointing. Brian believed he could make something of himself. He wanted his dad to be around long enough to witness it, and now he never would.

"I just hate that I lost him in the manner that I did," he says, "though to be honest, I lost him years before he passed."

Brian was angry. From his vantage point at the time, he thought Charles had let him down—and let his mother down. He knew only the sketchiest details of his father's war-torn past—that generation didn't discuss such things—and Brian was left to sort out questions that would never be fully answered.

"At the end of the day, he did the best he could with what he had," Brian says, shrugging. "It took me many years to realize that I had never walked a mile in his shoes, and basically all's forgiven. At the end of the day I wish he was still here."

At least he had his mom.

"Dad (Charles), Mom (Leah), and me at sister Flora's house in Troy, New York, in 1982. I was 26." —Brian

"When it comes down to the core of the matter, where did you find your strength, where did you find your foundation, where did you find your purpose? Leah Arlina Prout is where I found it."

Charles left practically nothing. The family enlisted the Veterans Administration to help pay for the funeral. And Brian's inheritance from his father was a gag shirt that read "International Bull Shippers."

It wasn't the only joke played on Brian that fall. Upon his return to Florida, he discovered that Arlen had reclaimed his job as the Hot Walker drummer. He had lost his dad, had lost his job, and was back in a city he was determined to leave. Brian Prout was one angry guy. He didn't have a lot of options.

But he called Kenny Kramer, a guitar player on the Lauderdale scene. Kenny's band, Heartbreak Mountain, had fired the drummer, who had a drug problem, so Brian's timing was great. He had a new gig. The band

Photograph by Jan Brannen

Brian back in his Heartbreak Mountain days in South Florida. Cahoots' in Jupiter, Florida, 1983.

was younger, was better looking, and dressed a little flashier than the Hot Walker boys. In short order, Heartbreak Mountain counted on a rhythm section that paired Brian on drums with bass player Jon Marcus, destined to become a member of Tim McGraw's Dancehall Doctors. Heartbreak Mountain became a force in South Florida.

Still, Lauderdale isn't quite Nashville, and Brian felt their only real future resided in Middle Tennessee. He convinced the rest of Heartbreak Mountain to join him on a trip in June 1983 to Fan Fair, an annual convention that attracts thousands of country fans to the fairgrounds in Music City for a series of concerts and the opportunity to have their pictures taken with many of the genre's bona fide stars.

"We're just bein' the geek tourists," Brian remembers. "We've got all our Fan Fair credentials, we're goin' around gettin' people's autographs and this and that, tryin' to meet people downtown, and we've got videos at the time and cassette tapes and stuff we'd been recording down in South Florida."

Fort Lauderdale was certainly better than Troy, but Nashville was even better than Florida. Lauderdale was bigger than his birthplace, but Brian's future as a country musician there was much the same: he could be, at best, a big fish in a small pond.

He started talking up Music City with his Heartbreak Mountain bandmates. Brian remembered his brother's advice to leave Troy if he intended to make it. That same bit of wisdom applied to this band. They needed to move to where the decision makers lived—put themselves in the same area code as the people who could change their lives.

"I didn't want to come to Nashville by myself as a drummer," Brian says. "I saw all the other drummers that were comin' into town with these other [solo] artists, and I had never been a sideman. I had never been somebody's drummer. I was the drummer *in* [a band], I was a full-blown member *of*—I had never played *for* somebody."

Brian's sales job worked. Heartbreak Mountain left Florida behind for an uncertain future in Nashville. They crammed five bodies into a two-bedroom duplex; the other four musicians got beds, while Brian slept on the couch. They picked up a job within just two weeks, playing the Western Room on Printers Alley downtown. It wasn't exactly glamorous. The club was tiny, and the stage was positioned behind the bar. To make matters worse, the pay was less than half what they'd made in Florida. The setup tested the band members' patience—some more than others.

"Mike Roberts was our lead singer at the time," Brian explains. "Mike was a very good-looking guy, a tremendous singer when he wanted to be. And Mike had an issue with the coke, and he had women just throwing themselves at him constantly. So we come to Nashville, and he wasn't here six, seven months and just started losin' it."

Homesick, Mike abandoned Heartbreak Mountain and headed back to Florida. Tragically, Mike got sucked back into the Lauderdale party scene and eventually lost his life to alcohol and cocaine.

In need of a new vocalist, Kenny Kramer and fellow band member Donny Allen focused on a duo back in Sanford, Florida, just north of Orlando. The Raybon Brothers were a solid bluegrass-gospel outfit, and Marty Raybon had a stunning voice. The opportunity to join an established band—even on the club circuit—in the shadow of Music Row was too much for Marty to pass up. He took the job and was soon a regular on the bandstand at the Western Room.

David Schulman, the owner of another Printers Alley club, Skull's Rainbow Room, was friends with the cast at *Hee Haw*, and Skull's brought a steady stream of visitors to the Alley from that TV show and other parts of the entertainment business. Many of them found their way to the Western Room: Buck Owens, Roy Clark, Roni Stoneman, *Hee Haw* producer Sam Lovullo, Marianne Rogers, Lulu Roman, songwriter Mack Vickery (author of the George Strait hit "The Fireman")—even the Judds.

"It was crazy times, but Marty was gettin' all the attention," Brian recalls.

That's not how things had run in Florida. There, Heartbreak Mountain had had its picture featured en masse in the local entertainment fliers. Here, people singled out the singer.

"That started to create a little tension in the band," Brian says. "I didn't care. That dude is standin' three feet in front of me. I'll ride your coattails to the top of the charts."

One particular evening, Bobby Braddock slumped into a chair along the mirrored wall at the Western Room. Bobby was already an established member of the Nashville Songwriters Hall of Fame. He'd won Song of the Year honors from both the Country Music Association and the Academy of Country Music for cowriting the George Jones hit "He Stopped Loving Her Today." He'd also penned Tammy Wynette's "D-I-V-O-R-C-E," John Anderson's "Would You Catch a Falling Star," and John Conlee's "I Don't Remember Loving You."

Brian insisted, against Marty's judgment, that they play "He Stopped Loving Her Today."

"In the middle of the song, Marty turns around to me, literally on the Western Room stage," Brian says. "Marty goes, 'He hates it. He hates it.'

"1986. One of my first shows with the Tennessee River Boys." —Brian

When we finished the song, Marty finished it with this long trill—he didn't sing it like George Jones; he sang it like Marty Raybon. Bobby Braddock just stood up and clapped. And when we finished the set, he came over to Marty. Two days later, Marty was singin' demos for Bobby Braddock at Tree Publishing."

Marty's good fortune became Heartbreak Mountain's cross. Marty quit the band, moved to Muscle Shoals in short order, and

fell in with another group of musicians in Alabama. By 1987, that band had found its way to the national charts under the name Shenandoah.

Heartbreak Mountain was "basically falling apart, much to my dismay," says Brian, who had come to "the realization that so much of it is centered around the lead singer. There was no real hard feelings on my part. I just thought, *Well, Marty, if you ever need a drummer . . .*"

In fact, another drummer gave Brian two introductions that would have a major impact on his life. Suzanne Elmer was one of the first people he met when Heartbreak Mountain first rolled into Nashville. She had a day job as a drummer out at the Opryland theme park and played at night at Faron Young's Country Junction, across Printers Alley from the Western Room. Suzanne introduced Brian to yet another female drummer, Nancy Given, who played the kit in Porter Wagoner's all-female band, the Right Combination. She and multi-instrumentalist Wanda Vick would go on to form Wild Rose, but in the meantime she hit it off with Brian, marrying him in 1986.

In the early part of that year, Suzanne helped him make another important connection. In later years, as a friend and real-estate agent, she would match him with the right condo. This time she patched him into a band she knew from Opryland. The Tennessee River Boys had lost their drummer, and, like Heartbreak Mountain, they had aspirations to land a deal with a Nashville record company.

George Bailey's dream was still alive.

chapter 7

GENE JOHNSON

Russ Harrington

*D*uring his tenure with the genre-busting Dave Bromberg Quartet, Gene Johnson performed in 1982 and again in '83 at prestigious Carnegie Hall in New York. The venue is one that causes many musicians to salivate, one that even non-musicians recognize as significant. After Gene first played at Carnegie, his dad was particularly interested in what it meant.

"Have you taken this country music—or whatever you play—up to the level of Carnegie Hall?" Vern Johnson asked his son.

"Or"—he winked—"is Carnegie Hall slippin' just a little bit?"

The memory elicits a tear from Gene. The Carnegie date is now just a nice footnote on his musical resume; his father, unfortunately, never got to see just how significant that resume would become.

Those two shows also have an appropriate connection to Gene's past. There's an old vaudeville joke in which a tourist asks someone in Manhattan, "How do you get to Carnegie Hall?" The answer: "Practice, man, practice."

If there's anything Vern Johnson taught his son, it was the importance of hard work, which is the essence of practice. The hard work that surrounded Gene during his youth was the never-ending toil that accompanies a family farm. Born in Jamestown, New York, on August 10, 1949, Gene was a mix of European descent. His great-grandfather had migrated to the U.S. from Sweden during the 1800s, while Nicholas McGrath—the father of Gene's mother, Olive—came from Ireland around the time of the American centennial. Farmwork was consuming, and it helped to have a big family to get it done—Olive was the eleventh of twelve children.

Even during the Roaring Twenties, as Gene's parents came of age, there was no TV—and barely any radio. Electricity hadn't reached rural homes, and the horse and buggy was still the primary mode of transportation. Entertainment was homespun, and music was a big part of it. In fact, it was music that brought Gene's mom and dad together in a story that sounds eerily like the "I'd start walkin' your way" tale of Diamond Rio's first hit, "Meet in the Middle."

Vern lived in Sugar Grove, Pennsylvania, just a mile south of the New York state border. He was dating one—maybe even two—of the three Alexander girls and would walk three miles to call on them at their farmhouse. Invariably, as he trudged the three miles back home in the dark, he would pass the McGrath house, bathed in lamplight and bustling with activity.

"The house was rockin', because he could hear all the music playing inside," Gene says. "My dad liked music, and actually he met my mother because of that very fact. He got to know one of her brothers well enough that he started to learn guitar from him, so my dad learned to play from my mother's family."

The Alexander sisters were soon forgotten, and the Johnson-McGrath household set up its own farm.

"One hundred fifty acres and all the work you wanted—or could stand," Gene chuckles.

His father took that work concept a step further. Vern spent nine hours a day as the foreman in a furniture factory, overseeing both the manufacture and design of wood furnishings. But his labor wasn't finished when he clocked out. He'd continue doing outdoor farm chores until the daylight disappeared—then it was off to the barn to continue working by lamp.

In addition to harvesting the crops and tending to the animals, the family—which included brother Dick, twelve years older than Gene; Fred, ten years his senior; and sister Hazel, who preceded Gene by five years—also made syrup, a complicated, time-consuming process. Gene picked up on the farming and syrup making, as well as the building and upkeep of the home.

"I learned all stages of construction from the foundation to the roof of houses, plus all the cabinet making and all that kind of stuff," he notes. "I've completely plumbed houses, I've completely put the electric in houses. You know, I mean, I can build you a house from the ground up and do every bit of the work."

"The Johnson kids. Hazel was mad that the boys all got haircuts for the picture, so she started cutting her own bangs. Dick, Fred, Hazel, me." —Gene

Gene's boyhood home always smelled incredible. His grandmother McGrath had died before her kids were grown, and his mother—beginning at age twelve—took over the baking duties at her house. Throughout the rest of her life, she baked bread, biscuits, pies, and cakes nearly every day.

Olive worked just as hard as her husband and wasn't above feeding the animals or picking up a pitchfork when the family was falling behind in its chores. The Johnson parents set an obvious tone for the family, willing to do whatever it took—no matter how unglamorous it might be—to meet their needs.

"If it needed done, you went out and did it," Gene says. "There were so many things that I didn't like doing. The thing about it, when you do it—whether you're cleaning out a septic tank by hand, which is not a pleasant job, by the way—if you literally jump into it and you do it, you know, you realize you can. You can do this. It doesn't have to have the big circle with the cross through it. I think that's a good attitude to have through life: it's not that tough—you can do this."

That attitude certainly helped Gene's father build relationships in the community. Vern was "easygoing, liked by everybody, as far as I could tell," Gene says. "He had a good nature about him. He was always willing to help the neighbors—we lived in that time, you know, neighbors helped the neighbors. If you couldn't get your crops in out of the fields, all of the neighbors came over and helped you."

Young Gene figured he would spend his adult life as a farmer, too, but—thanks in great part to that musical bond between the Johnsons and the McGraths—he developed another interest on the bandstand. Vern called square dances and played the fiddle. Gene soon joined his brothers, Dick and Fred, in the band when he was a mere four years of age.

"Mandolin," he says, "was the smallest instrument we had, so that's what I got."

Within just a few years after Gene began playing, his brothers enrolled at Cornell University in Ithaca, New York, where they met a young musician named Bob Mavian, who played the same three-finger banjo style that Earl Scruggs played in his bluegrass duo with Lester Flatt. Dick and Fred were fascinated with the genre, and their interests quickly rubbed off on Gene, who played the same instrument—mandolin—as Bill Monroe, Flatt & Scruggs's original employer in the Blue Grass Boys.

"My brothers had a few records, and then we were searching, trying to find more, and I learned about Monroe and all these people," Gene recalls. "Bluegrass just took off with me. Learning bluegrass back then was definitely a little tougher. I mean, the only way you had to learn was to set that needle back on the record, you know, [so I] wore out the records."

By the time he was ten, Gene was also worn out on the concept of becoming a farmer.

"What really hit home for me at one point in time was when one of our neighbors got just deathly ill," he says. "He had a lot of cows to milk,

117

and so, of course, we were down helpin' him out. Even though we were there to help milk and all that, he was still out doin' it, sick—so sick he should've been in a hospital.

"But he couldn't stand to have all his neighbors out there workin' for him and him not be doin' somethin', so he's out there workin' too. And it kinda hit home with me, *You should be in bed at least.* I realized when you're on a farm, no matter what, the work needs done and you're gonna do it. That kinda scared me away from bein' a farmer right there."

Around 1959 or '60, Gene went up to Ithaca with his brothers for the weekend. They were playing bluegrass with another pair of brothers—Bill and Dick Smith—and the Johnsons stopped by Bill's house one evening. Bill's daughter, June, was immediately taken with Gene, who was two years older than she was.

"She swears that that first time she met me, she decided I was the one she was gonna marry," Gene says. "She's been in love with me since then."

Never mind that they lived two hundred miles apart.

"Me and Sean (a wonderful friend, and a great coon dog)." —Gene

As fate would have it, that changed in very short order. Both Bill and Dick Smith moved to Sugar Grove, and they put Gene to work playing in the clubs, despite the fact that he was a mere thirteen years of age. His whatever-it-takes mentality immediately worked to everyone's advantage.

"We were the only bluegrass musicians in the area," Gene says with a shrug, "so if they needed a bass player, I played bass. If they needed a mandolin player, I played mandolin—whatever was called for, you know, I'd go out and I'd play. And I became the tenor singer, too, because I was young and I had a high voice."

Even on the rural border that straddled New York and Pennsylvania—eighty-five miles from Buffalo, the nearest major city—Gene was out of step with his teenage peers. In 1964, the Beatles led the British Invasion, a musical wave that profoundly changed the prism through which pop music was viewed. Gene was, at the time anyway, entirely unimpressed. He was much more interested in Jim & Jesse, the Osborne Brothers, and the Country Gentlemen.

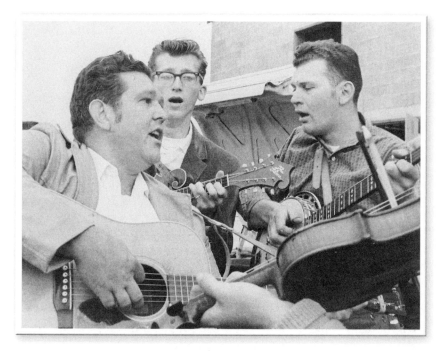

"I was an honorary Smith Brothers. Parking lot practice before a show at Bristol Center, New York, circa 1966. Bill on guitar, Dick on banjo." —Gene

"Prom night for me and June. I had to borrow the jacket from Hazel's husband, Dave."
—Gene

"I sang in the choir in high school, and our choir director did a thing once where he wanted everybody to bring in some of their favorite music, and I took in the Osborne Brothers," Gene recalls. "Wow, the faces that all my classmates and he made as they played that, it was pretty funny. Even though I could be in the choir and sing with them, I was just off in another entirely different world."

Gene's world, in fact, provided him the kind of education that can't be obtained in school. He'd play in the bars at night—always with a note from his parents indicating that one of the guys in the band was authorized to be his guardian for the evening.

But that led to many late nights, and it was often tough for Gene to get through classes the next day. He still got A's and B's in math, but rarely picked up much more than a C in English—and didn't really care. It wasn't music.

Homework took even more of a backseat when he started dating June during his last couple of years in high school.

In spite of his grades, Gene enrolled in college in Oswego, north of Syracuse along Lake Ontario. He majored in industrial arts—a direct route to teaching high school shop classes—but once again, he spent his evenings playing bluegrass music, this time in a band featuring a lead singer, Freddie Bartlett, whose voice was sweet, but unusually high.

"It pushed me hard to sing tenor to him," Gene says. "As a result, my range went up workin' with him when I was in college."

Roanoke, Virginia, hosted the first multiday bluegrass festival during Labor Day weekend in 1965. The concept sprang up in locations around the country, such as Bean Blossom, Indiana; Ocala, Florida; Reidsville, North Carolina; and even the Mall in Washington DC. Gene had attended plenty of festivals and found it easy to make friends with some of the professionals on the circuit. Especially when they figured out he had some talent.

"As bluegrassers, people held you in higher regard, but they also expected that they could walk up and talk to you," Gene says. "Back at all those early festivals, you pulled in and you had the musicians area that you parked in—maybe not. Some festivals didn't even have that. You kinda parked out where everybody else was parked. People [would] come and mingle around at whatever vehicle you had. It's very much less formal than what it gets to with the country music fan, where all of a sudden you have security just to keep people away from you."

Gene and his brother, Fred, worked much of 1970 as the Johnson Brothers. The act included a fiddler named Jeff Wisor who continued to play with Gene in several different groups through the years.

The Johnson Brothers, 1971. "We would spend two months in Montana that year. Zero degrees was a heat wave. (Me, my brother Fred, and Jeff Wisor)." —Gene

One of his professional friends was fellow mandolin player Jimmy Gaudreau, then a member of the DC-based Country Gentlemen. Cliff Waldron—a rival bandleader noted for adapting such pop songs as Ike and Tina Turner's "Proud Mary" and Manfred Mann's "Fox on the Run" for bluegrass consumption—was in search of a tenor singer and multi-instrumentalist for his band, New Shades of Grass, and Jimmy suggested Gene.

In early '71, Gene took the job and lived in several DC-area locations, periodically going back to visit June and his family in Sugar Grove. For a time he shared an apartment with Cliff, who'd gone through a recent breakup; then he moved into a converted firehouse with New Shades banjo player Jimmy Arnold in the Old Town section of

Alexandria, Virginia, where they still slid down the pole from the second floor to the first.

Finally, June relocated in '72 and shared a home with Gene about sixty-five miles outside of DC in Charles Town, West Virginia. It soon became inconvenient. She was pregnant and there were no hospitals within a reasonable distance. They moved again to an apartment complex in District Heights, Maryland, where plenty of young, financially struggling couples were trying to forge their new lives.

Many were less successful in that endeavor than Gene and June; the two of them sometimes got their entertainment by watching out the window as the other couples squared off in the courtyard, yelling and haggling—sometimes throwing things—until the police finally came to break it up. The scene would resonate with Gene years later when Diamond Rio recorded a song called "Redneck Love."

The Johnsons had their first daughter, Callie, on August 29, 1972, but that wasn't the only change in store at that time. Having recorded a couple of albums with Cliff, Gene accepted a job with Eddie Adcock, a former member of the Country Gentlemen. John Duffey, who'd sang the tenor in the

Baby Callie. "Still trying to comprehend fatherhood." —Gene

Gentlemen's classic mid-'60s lineup, was a heavy influence on Gene's style of harmony, and that made Gene a natural vocal partner in Eddie's new band, the IInd Generation.

Gene spent less than two years total in the DC area, but his residence had a huge effect on his vocational psyche. It might not have had quite the national recognition as a music hub that New York, Los

Kenji Mitsuta

John Duffey and Gene Johnson. "John was very influential on my singing style." —Gene

Angeles, or Nashville maintained, but Washington had its own significant club scene. Emmylou Harris, Bill and Taffy Danoff (the authors of John Denver's "Take Me Home, Country Roads"), the Gentlemen, and the Seldom Scene were among the artists who called it home.

DC was also an essential stopover for folk and bluegrass musicians on tour. It was where Emmylou first met Chris Hillman and her mentor, Gram Parsons, and it was a frequent stomping ground for Bill Monroe and Ralph Stanley. Gene got to spend significant time with Ricky Skaggs and Keith Whitley for the first time when they dropped in at Ruby's in Woodbridge, Virginia, as members of Ralph's Clinch Mountain Boys.

Don Light managed the IInd Generation out of Nashville, and Eddie decided to move the band to Music City at the end of '72. June and Callie needed some stability. Gene had no idea how he'd fare financially in Tennessee, so they moved back to Sugar Grove. They had little or no money, and Christmas was approaching. So with Callie nearing four months of age, in lieu of a present, Gene Johnson gave June Smith his last name. They finally got married, as June had believed they would the first time she laid eyes on him on that Christmas Eve so long ago.

"Remember," he says, "this is still kind of the hippie days, so, you know, when she was pregnant, we decided we wouldn't get married just because she was pregnant. We got married a few months afterward, so [we could say] we weren't forced into it."

Gene and IInd Generation drummer Michael Clem shared an apartment in Madison, north of Nashville. Gene sent money home to June when there was any left over. And he burned up the highways—and a few cars as well—when the tours broke, so he could spend time with his family.

On July 22, 1975, a second daughter, Mattie, arrived. For the second time, a newborn coincided with a new band affiliation. This time Gene said good-bye to the IInd Generation in a huff after a confrontation with Eddie during the Fourth of July weekend at a festival in Berryville, Virginia. They'd played a late set the previous night, and Gene arrived at the Berryville concert site early enough to go on, but not early enough for Eddie's taste. Eddie was berating his wife, Martha, but Gene quickly realized the anger was misplaced.

"It was one of those flare-up-of-the-moment things," says Gene, who remains friends with Eddie more than three decades later. "He was arguin' with her, and I said, 'Hey, if you're mad at me, don't be hollerin' at her.' And then we went back and forth, and first thing you know, I packed up my mandolin and went back to the parking area."

Jimmy Gaudreau, whom Gene had replaced in Eddie's band, happened to be on stage with another act at the time and ably filled in.

Night Sun. "Lots of miles for little pay. (Butch Amiot, me, Dick Smith, Scott McElhaney, Jeff Wisor)." —Gene

Gene, meanwhile, went into recruiting mode, and before the festival was over, the formation of a new group called Night Sun was in the making. Members would include II Generation fiddler Jeff Wisor, bass player Butch Amiot, singer/guitarist Scott McElhaney, and banjo player Dick Smith (June's uncle). Butch stayed with the band only six months before moving on, replaced by II Generation's Johnny Castle. After a couple of years, Gene tired of chewing up the road between Music City and Sugar Grove and decided to hang it up.

He moved back to New York and started overseeing the renovation of older houses for a real estate speculator in the Jamestown area. In short order he was also back in the clubs two or three nights a week with a blue-grass trio called Sun Mountain, featuring David Engstrom and former Night Sun cohort Butch Amiot. By holding down two jobs in New York, Gene made a decent living and had more time with June and the kids.

But the road still tugged at Gene—more than he realized. J. D. Crowe,

© Señor McGuire

"JD Crowe and the New South (promo shot), 1980. *Top*: Keith Whitley, Steve Bryant. *Bottom*: me, JD Crowe, Bobby Sloane." —Gene

one of bluegrass music's legends, called in 1979 with a job offer. The lead singer was a pretty good one too: Keith Whitley. Two weeks later, Gene was on the road again. He didn't move to Lexington, Kentucky—J. D.'s home base—but commuted once again from Sugar Grove, staying at different band members' houses in Kentucky, including Keith's home, where the two would stay up nights singing harmony to old Lefty Frizzell songs.

In '81 came the gig with Bromberg, a musically diverse soul who shifted between bluegrass, folk, and the blues. He encouraged Gene to take chances on other instruments, and he paid him well for the era: two hundred dollars a night and air transportation, rather than bus travel.

"I was introduced to completely different kinds of music," Gene says. "He was very eclectic, and we would play a lot of the time as a trio or quartet and mainly bluegrass instrumentation, but not necessarily all bluegrass tunes. But then we'd also go out as a twelve-piece band with a four-piece horn section, and I'd be playin' electric guitar, which I had never done before, but David had the faith in me and said, 'Oh, you can do it.' He'd sit down with me and show me some stuff and really was encouraging to me, had complete faith in my ability to do things, which was very good for me."

Gene's tenure with Bromberg coincided roughly with the emergence of Ricky Skaggs as a country star. Ricky had his first hits in 1981, playing mandocaster—a hybrid of the mandolin and electric guitar—and grafting Stanley Brothers harmonies onto mainstream country textures.

Bromberg, in contrast, was scaling back his tour dates, which put a dent once more in Gene's income. Keith Whitley, Gene's former bandmate, moved to Tennessee in 1984 with an eye toward shifting from bluegrass to country. And he bugged Gene on occasion to do the same.

"Keith would call me up and say, 'You need to be in Nashville,'" Gene recalls. "One of the things he used to say was, 'If Ricky can make it here, you can make it here.' And I'm like, 'Keith, you seem to have a lot more faith in me than I do.' He said, 'No, I'm not kiddin'. I know both of you.

"This shot was taken during a European tour in 1983. Me, Butch Amiot, David Bromberg (back), Bill Kraushaur (front), and Jeff Wisor." —Gene

I know you can make it here.' So he's one of the reasons that I moved down. He was almost insistent that I get out, get away from small-town Pennsylvania and move to where the music was at."

In '84, Gene auditioned for a job with Steve Wariner that went instead to Steve's brother, Terry. But June got a job as the office manager and bookkeeper for High-Tech Service, a repair shop for expensive electronic gear. With Gene still doing limited Bromberg dates, they figured it was time to take the plunge.

"I had realized along the way that I was getting toward the backside of viability, age-wise," Gene says. "I was already thirty-six. I had started out as a really little kid. I'd always been the youngest guy in the band, and somewhere along the way, it had started to turn a little bit where I wasn't any longer the youngest. At thirty-six, I obviously wasn't the oldest guy, but it had started to occur to me that if I'm gonna get into anything worthwhile, I'm gonna have to try to hook up with some younger people."

1983. "Festival in the northeast. (David, Butch Amiot, me)." —Gene

He was tested even while he prepared to move. While packing boxes at the Sugar Grove farmhouse, Gene got a call from Charlie Waller with the Country Gentlemen, offering a regular gig. It was tempting—he liked Charlie, liked the music—but he was determined to give Nashville a try. If it didn't work after a few years, he could always shift back into bluegrass. Gene turned down the gig and left Sugar Grove with June and the girls, departing on Callie's thirteenth birthday.

For a while, Nashville was cruel. Not a lot of gigs came his way. He was shocked when he hit the road with Ricky for a weekend, only to find out the pay was a hundred dollars a night, half of what the less-in-demand Bromberg had paid.

June got a better job after a couple of years, becoming the office manager for Masterfonics, a mastering facility in the heart of Music Row, where artists and producers finalized their recordings before they went off to the pressing plant to be distributed to the public. In a rather odd twist of fate, the building was on the corner across the street from CBS, an office that had been converted from the old Columbia Recording Studios, where such acts as George Jones, Marty Robbins, Johnny Cash, and Bob Dylan—one of Bromberg's former associates—had made some of their key records. Gene felt like an outsider, and his wife was working smack dab in the middle of the industry he wanted to be part of. He took work in cabinetry to bring in some extra money, and he even built speaker cabinets at Masterfonics, just around the block from the Musicians Union.

Gene's mom, Olive, had died in 1983, and his dad was suffering from Parkinson's disease. Vern moved down to Nashville in early 1986 and lived with Gene for about four years before they finally had to have him hospitalized. It was good to have Dad around, but it created a bit of a burden on June and the girls. When Gene was out making music, Vern still needed attention—and his illness became increasingly difficult for untrained caretakers.

"The Birchmere in Arlington, Virginia. JD Crowe and the New South: me, JD, and Keith." —Gene

Keith, meanwhile, was making it. He had several hits, including "Ten Feet Away" and "Homecoming '63," shortly after Gene's arrival. He called Gene whenever he could. One particular day he made a point of telling Gene about recording "I Never Go Around Mirrors," one of the Lefty Frizzell songs they used to harmonize on during their years with J. D. Crowe. Whitey Shafer, who cowrote the original, had written an extra verse for Keith, who just had to share the good news with his friend.

"Keith sang me the new verse for the song over the phone, and you could tell he was just giddy," Gene recalls. "He said, 'I went in and cut it today. On my way in to the studio, I stopped at the cemetery and sang it to Lefty first.' I've never known anyone who admired Lefty more than Keith. Later, Keith had Lefty's brother, Allen, come in and sing the harmony. It was great."

Though things developed slowly for Gene, he didn't waver from his plan to get into country. He hadn't caved in when the offer came from the Country Gentlemen. And he didn't crack when he received a phone call from the Tennessee River Boys, whose name had all the earmarks of another bluegrass band. Fortunately, the River Boys' Jimmy Olander was persistent and called a second time. Gene would get the chance to audition for them. It was his road to success, though neither Keith—nor Vern—would witness it.

chapter 8

DANA WILLIAMS

Russ Harrington

*O*utside of death and divorce, few things are more traumatizing than a move to a new city. The change in culture is almost always a shock to the system, but in the best circumstances, it means a new and better life.

So it was for Dana Williams, who had no control over his family's move from his native Ohio to Nashville when he was eleven years old. The relocation put him in the perfect city to build his future career as a musician, but it was a change of scenery he had no way of knowing he would need. And it was a move he might never have made on his own.

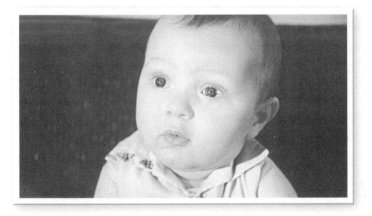

"3 months old and can't decide to cry or not." —Dana

"Resting from trying to walk." —Dana

"I just don't know that I was the type of person that could've done that," he confesses. "I was too much of a home kid, too much a mama's boy—whatever you wanna call it, I was too much of that. And I don't see myself jumping in whatever car I could afford at the time and headin' for another state and leaving my family and livin' on my own. I just don't see that happening."

"But," he adds, "you never know."

Dana never had to find out. His father, Maurice, had worked for more than two decades at the McCall's printing plant in the Dayton area. The plant produced *Redbook* and *Glamour* magazines, as well as the catalogs for McCall's, a company that provided sewing patterns for homemakers to follow in making clothes for their families. In an earlier era—one that held sway when Dana was born May 22, 1961—sewing was part of a housewife's typical role, though that function became antiquated with the rise of the two-income family.

Similarly, the McCall's printing job became outdated as computers changed the industry. Dana's daddy created metal plates that were used to

Left: "A man came through the neighborhood with a horse and cowboy outfit and someone made me take a picture. It was 1966, I was 5 and the horse was named Jack!" *Right:* "Daddy got a new camera. Very possible this was my first photo shoot. 1 1/2 years old." —Dana

Top left: "Just got home from church and I am ready for business. Five years old." *Top right:* "I still have that tricycle today, sitting right beside of Jacob's in my garage. Can't reach the pedals again." *Bottom left:* "Lawrence Welk had nothing on me, baby! Five years old and already digging the groove." *Bottom right:* "On the lake, groovy shades, a *Reds* cap, and a Barq's red crème soda! Just don't get no better than that in 1965!"
—Dana

guide the printing of pages for the McCall's catalog and a variety of other magazines. As technology changed, those plates became old-fashioned, and the printing companies that failed to adapt eventually saw their plants closed. When the bad news came down for the Williams family, they took a brief vacation to visit Dana's uncles in Nashville.

They weren't typical relatives. Bobby and Sonny were well known to bluegrass fans and Grand Ole Opry listeners as the Osborne Brothers. Kentucky born, they'd formed a partnership in Dayton in 1953 and started recording in Nashville the following year. In 1964 they joined the Opry, becoming one of only a handful of bluegrass acts on the venerable radio show's roster; and three years later, their recording of "Rocky Top" became one of the few staples of the genre to gain a foothold outside of bluegrass.

The Osbornes had come back to Dayton to pay a visit around the time Dana was ten or eleven, and that visit had lit a fire he'd previously let burn out. Dana's mother and sister played a lot of Elvis Presley music around the house, and he had started playing the snare drum. His parents even signed him up for lessons, though after the second one Dana shrugged off the music, preferring instead to hang out with his friends and ride his bike around the neighborhood, a Pete Rose baseball card ticking in the spokes. The Osbornes, however, turned his head. His uncles weren't the only musical folks in the family—even Dana's cousin, Wynn, Bobby's son, had bona fide talent.

"He stayed with us and all of a sudden he started playin' bass, and brother, he was really playin'," Dana recalls. "And then he went from bass to guitar, and he ended up finally landing on banjo. Wynn Osborne, he's probably one of the finest banjo players to ever come around. And what does he do [now]? Works for some place down in Florida, doesn't even play banjo anymore. And I'm like, *Wow.*"

So when the Williams family went to visit the Osbornes after the printing plant closed, Dana got to spend more time with Wynn. And Maurice Williams decided to check out the employment market.

"Daddy made a few phone calls, and he called [the morning paper] the *Tennessean,* asking if there might be some work," Dana explains. "They said, 'Hey, man, can you come to work tomorrow?' He said, 'No, but I can be here a week from tomorrow.' So we hightailed it home, and he packed up that camper and came back to Nashville and went to work at the *Tennessean*."

Louise Williams, Dana's mother, stayed in Ohio and packed the rest of their belongings while the house in suburban Beavercreek sold. Maurice came back to Dayton on weekends and pitched in until they found a buyer, and the family headed to Music City on Thanksgiving Day 1972. The job at the *Tennessean* lasted only six months at most

"This is what I got for my 11th birthday and I bet it's still in Mother and Daddy's attic." —Dana

before computers once again forced a job change, but it was long enough that the Williams were able to get over the culture shock of moving to the mid-South. They never returned to their original hometown.

"When I got here as an eleven-year-old, I was embarrassed to call anybody ma'am or sir," Dana says. "You didn't call anybody ma'am or sir [in Ohio]—no, that wasn't how you were taught. But boy, you got here and you either called those teachers ma'am or sir or you got a paddlin'."

The paddling wasn't nearly as intimidating as he might have received in Dayton. The Nashville school system had specified the number of swats the administrator gave for certain offenses, so there was always a limit to the punishment.

"In Ohio, you got a whippin'," he says. "There wasn't no counting. You got here and you get three licks for this; that'll get ya two licks. I'm like, *Two? That's it?*"

There was a weird language barrier too. The kids would ask about his motor, and Dana figured they were referring to an engine. In fact, they were talking about his motorcycle.

"Oh," he said, "you mean my cycle."

"Cycle?" they laughed. "You mean like a popsicle?"

When the neighbors asked if he was "sweet on" the girl across the street, Dana was completely confused. Despite the weirdness of the language, there was something about Nashville that made the transition comparatively easy, even for a preteen who'd left every friend he'd ever known. Ohio was soon a blip in his past.

"I have been Tennessee'd," Dana announces with more than a hint of drawl.

It helped to have relatives in town, and with the family's proximity to the Osbornes, Dana's interest in music became obsessive. He played his snare right along with the recordings of Sonny and Bobby, as well as the music of Elvis, who had reclaimed some of his youthful swagger in the summer before the Williams family moved. "Burning Love" was the rockingest hit Elvis had had in a decade or so, and even though he was of another generation, he'd been cool enough to worm his way into the pop charts right alongside Three Dog Night and Chicago. Dana imagined it was just a matter of time before he could worm his way into a gig.

"I was going to be Elvis's drummer," he says. "Ronnie Tutt was just the king to me."

His parents got Dana a full drum kit as a Christmas present within a couple of years of arriving in Tennessee, and as soon as he got home from school, Dana was usually seated at the kick drum, doing his best King

Tutt impressions. He could have pursued some other extracurricular activities, but there wasn't much point.

"I had football coaches comin' to the house to talk my mother and my daddy into lettin' me play football for the city or for school," he says. "They said, 'Hey, man, he has no interest in that at all.' I was a big boy, you know. 'He has no interest in that. Listen [to him] out there.' All I was doin' was playin' 'Blue Moon of Kentucky' and 'Roll Muddy River' and seein' how fast I could play drums and all this good stuff."

"I was 15 here and convinced 'Elvis' was calling any day!" —Dana

Wynn and Dana entered a talent contest in Hendersonville with a bare-bones act. Wynn played the melody of a song they'd written on his bass, and Dana accompanied on snare. The act was so poorly conceived they didn't even get past the first round. But a year or two later, they expanded to a trio—Wynn shifted to banjo, Dana took up bass, and another friend took over on drums—and gave a three-song instrumental performance in the parking lot at Hill's grocery store.

Playing for an audience and in a group was fun. They became more serious about it and upped the ante by bringing in yet another friend to play rhythm guitar and sing, emulating as best they could the Osborne Brothers. Dana had wanted to stay on drums—how else could he become Ronnie Tutt? But he'd moved to bass for the sake of the band. Once he had familiarized himself with the instrument, he realized it had a unique place in the sonic structure of the group. As the lowest-pitched melodic instrument, it created the foundation for all the chord progressions and vocals they produced. At the same time, the bass was a key partner with the drums in setting the rhythmic tone for the whole unit.

"The Nashville Cousins: Wynn Osborne, Richard Lombardo, me, and Tony Morgan. Burksville, KY." —Dana

"I really liked the sound the bass gave a band," Dana says. "It sounded [one way] without it, and then when the bass came in, it sounded so full and so powerful. The rhythmic stuff was still there, so my background with drums really came in handy."

On a handful of occasions, the group was booked on Ralph Emery's local morning TV show—the same program the Judds would use, beginning in 1980, to gain attention in Nashville. The schedule required Dana to get up around 3:00 AM, do a few songs live, then head off to school, where his classmates were quick to talk up his mini-celebrity status, even if they didn't quite understand what he was doing.

"When you're a young kid playin' bluegrass like that, other kids, they just don't get it," he says.

Not that bluegrass was all he knew. Dana started listening to mainstream country music—Ronnie Milsap, Merle Haggard—and he was just as interested as the other kids in the pop music of the time, including Chicago and Toto.

He made no plans for college—no plans for anything, really, except to play music—"a recipe for disaster, if I've ever seen it," he says. But his plan started working within two months of graduation. In July 1979, Jeff Jared—a guitarist who would later play lead for Darryl Worley— recruited Dana to play in the Tim Gillis Band. Freddy Fender had hired the group's regular drummer, and they needed someone to jump in for a six-week run in Stillwater, Oklahoma. The gig was worth $250 weekly, though he'd have to pay lodging expenses out of that. With two guys sleeping in a room at a cheap hotel, it would still clear about $200. After food, Dana still might make $150.

It was definitely an adventure. Dana had never been away from his parents that long, never been in a bar before, never even been on a plane. Suddenly he had to do all of that, and it began with a solo flight from Nashville.

He was, he admits, "freaked out—eighteen years old, I was a big boy, scared to death, and I set down beside some little kid. He couldn't have been more than eight or nine, and he's travelin' by himself. I'm sittin' there shakin'. And he looked up at me, and he goes, 'You look like Elvis.' I said, 'Huh? *Elvis?*' That started our conversation, and that little kid talked me through that flight. I've thought about that since—that little kid is what moved me that step."

There were plenty more steps to take in short order. Jeff met him at the Tulsa airport in a van. Dana crawled in among four other complete strangers and headed west to Stillwater for their standing engagement at the Sundowner Lounge. Whatever fear Dana encountered on the plane was nothing compared to the terror awaiting him in that little country bar. The drummer he was replacing had three more nights to play, so Dana brought along a pen and a notebook to prep himself for the band's set.

"I went into that club, and first thing I see is that bar and all those bottles of liquor," he laughs, "and I'm thinkin', *People's gonna be shot, knifed, hung, everything in here. I know it. Tonight!* It was the worst thoughts that a kid could have, so I went and found me a table in the corner and set in the corner where nobody could come [up] behind to knife me. I could see it comin', and I sit there and watched, listened to them play. And I remember the waitresses wore these little red outfits with their boobs pushed up, real short skirts. I could hardly look at 'em, you know. This guy's laying at the bar like you see on TV, and this is awful. I was just freaked out."

The six-week trip was painful. Dana missed his parents, missed his house, missed Nashville. But he got an education and somehow made it through.

"In that six-week period, I saw so many people passed out and fights started and all this stuff," he says. "Oh, my. Still to this day, I don't understand it, but you know what? I've learned there's just things in life you won't ever understand, and I'm sure there's things about me nobody understands."

The Gillis gig didn't end after six weeks. He stayed with the band through the end of the year, adjusting to the road and to the bars, even though he resisted any cajoling by his bandmates or the patrons to sample the liquor. In fact, even by his midforties, he hadn't taken a sip of alcohol.

"I'd see these people all drunked up and layin' on top of car hoods, throwin' up and this and that," he says sarcastically, "and I'm like, *Mmmmm, good. Boy, I want in on that!*"

"August 25, 1979, in Kirksville, Missouri. Taken by Mother." —Dana

"I never, *ever* had the desire to want to take a drink of alcohol," he adds, "and I never wanted to smoke any kind of substance. I did try a cigarette and thought it was the worst thing I'd ever put in my mouth in my life, but I never wanted to do any kind of drug or any kind of altering medications whatsoever. I never had the want to ever attempt it, and I also never wanted to be around it."

That made Dana a rather unusual musician, though his penchant for nightlife fit the job description well. Even when he didn't have a gig, he stayed out until early morning with several friends from Hendersonville. In the winter they passed the nights at a twenty-four-hour bowling alley. In the summer they turned on the lights at a tennis court and played

"My first time to play the Opry. July 5, 1980, with Jimmy "C" Newman and Cajun Country." —Dana

until the sun came up. They could get burgers in the wee hours of the morning at the Krystal in Madison or drive all the way to the airport and play video games and pinball at the game room.

"We was all so ugly that girls was never an issue," he insists. "So it was just a bunch of dudes out not wantin' to go to bed, is about all that it amounted to."

After the job with the Gillis Band, Dana was determined to play bass. He got plenty of calls to do club gigs as a drummer—there weren't a lot of guys who could sit at the kit *and* sing harmony—but he routinely turned them down, trying to steer his way to the instrument he really wanted to play.

Jeff Jared picked up a job with Little Jimmy Dickens, and Dana accompanied him periodically to the Grand Ole Opry. Ray Kirkland, who'd previously played with the Osborne Brothers, was looking for someone to take over bass in Jimmy C. Newman's band, and he got Dana an audition. He did okay on the bass, but his ability to sing harmony earned him the gig. Dana debuted with Jimmy C on July 3, 1980. He made his first appearance on the Opry the next day.

"About 1981. You may see Marty Roe wearing this same shirt at any given show. They don't make 'em like that any more! Wade Benson Landry, me, Jimmy C, and Ken Albert back there on steel." —Dana

In less than a year, Dana had taken his first plane flight, played his first club, and completed his first tour. Now he was performing on the best-known show in country music history.

"Here I stand, shakin' again on the stage of the Grand Ole Opry," he says. "That was a cool moment."

For the next thirty months, Dana performed in Jimmy C's band, Cajun Country, which included steel player Terry Wendt. Terry pulled

"These shirts got burnt up in a bus fire, *bummer*! They were just so shiny! Me playing a bass solo on the song 'In the Mood.' Ray Kirkland and me, 1981." —Dana

double duty on the Opryland grounds, since he was a member of the *Country Music USA* show at the Roy Acuff Theater. The band included

a guitar player named Jimmy Olander, whom Dana would bump into periodically through the years on Nashville's club scene. Within a couple of years, Dana would hang out at another Opryland production—a group called the Tennessee River Boys.

For a while touring with Jimmy C was exciting. Dana saw parts of the U.S. he'd never experienced before—"I went to Louisiana for the first time and learned that it's a complete country in itself"—and

"Trying my best to hear those monitors! Me and the Country Bumpkin 'Cal Smith,' 1983." —Dana

performed in shows that featured other artists whose music he'd covered in the clubs, including George Jones and Doc Watson.

Dana spent seven or eight months with fiddler Vassar Clements, then picked up work with Cal Smith, whose "Country Bumpkin" had been an award-winning number-one hit about a decade before. Cal's peak period had subsided about five years before, but his songs were still more current than Jimmy C's, and Dana could tell the difference in the crowd's reaction. He then took a gig with Daryl Pillow, but after four-plus years of steady touring, the road no longer held any real fascination.

"I was fed up with it all," Dana remembers. "I came home and said, *'Man, I ain't playin' no more of these dumps. I've had it.'*"

He hadn't planned on doing anything *but* playing music, so there weren't a lot of options back in Hendersonville. He took a job delivering flowers for Claudine Brown's Florists, determined to forge a more normal life and put the music thing behind him. He'd barely been away from the scene for two months, though, when the first call came in.

"You wanna come out and play with us? We're only working on Saturday nights."

"Well, I guess I could come out on Saturdays."

Saturday expanded to Friday and Saturday. Then he picked up a gig on Sunday and Monday at the Starlight Lounge, and suddenly Dana had a forty-hour job *plus* club work that kept him out until three or four in the morning. Claudine, who owned the flower shop, was understanding—she'd call him in the morning after she got an order and ask him to come in and never seemed agitated by his tardiness.

Where the gigs with the Opry stars had been grounded solely in country music, the club work had a much wider span, and Dana appreciated the variety.

"In Nashville, you play all styles of music," he says. "A lot of times people think there's just country music here, and that ain't true. At that time, man, we was doin' everything from Whitney Houston to George Jones to Simply Red to Vern Gosdin. We were doin' it all."

Sometimes the places were packed, the people were getting into the music, and the whole thing was a blast. Other times the club would be crawling with drunks paying no attention whatsoever. Even worse were the times when the bar was empty. The band still had to play the set, just in case a customer or two might wander in and jump-start the night.

"If nothing else does it, that in itself will throw it right in your face that, man, you don't know how to do anything else, or at this juncture, you'd be doing it!" Dana laughs. "That's just a big ol' bummer, is what that is. And you know what? It's just part of it. In the musicians' world, you just looked at it that it's paid rehearsal. But if you're gonna rehearse, you'd definitely like to be rehearsin' something new instead of doin' 'He Stopped Loving Her Today' again—over and over again."

Dana was being tugged in two different directions—the late-night music and the conventional flower shop. Neither of them paid well, but he was making more money from music and having a better time. He quit the floral business and pushed to get the band a few more gigs. They ended up back out at the Opry, this time backing "Satin Sheets" singer Jeanne Pruett.

Through it all, Dana continued to live in his parents' house. Without alcohol consumption or drug issues clouding the relationship, he felt none of the antagonism that most twenty-somethings harbor toward their parents. Even when he slept in until 2:00 PM, which was pretty much every weekend, Maurice and Louise never grilled him about his hours.

Marriage, however, eventually got him out of the house. He wed Lisa in 1986. There was no transition period to get used to life away from Mom and Dad. No time in which he was the sole adult in his home. One day he lived with his parents; the next day he was married and suddenly responsible for himself, a house, and a wife.

"I remember laying there on my wedding night," he says. "I was laying there awake, she was layin' there asleep, and I'm lookin' at her, thinkin' to myself, *What have I done? What have I done?*"

Within a few years Dana decided it was time once again to quit the music grind. He had a wife, a home, and bills; the measly pay made it difficult to justify the weird hours. He decided to enroll in an electronics school in Hartsville, about an hour east. He drove out and picked up some registration forms and borrowed a textbook from Ron Hogan, the steel player from the Tim Gillis Band, who'd already gone through the program.

The papers were lying on the table when the phone rang. It was Jimmy Olander, the guy he'd met eight or nine years before when he was working with Jimmy C. Newman. Jimmy O was with the Tennessee River Boys, they were auditioning for a bass player who could sing harmony, and they had a TV booking on *Nashville Now*.

Dana couldn't quite resist it. He agreed to come down to Brian Prout's garage and try out for the job, promising Lisa all the while that it was just a one-time thing. He wasn't going to stay in music. He was going to electronics school, and they were going to make a new and better life.

chapter 9

WILD RIDE

With the addition of Dana Williams, the Tennessee River Boys had picked up the missing member they needed for the *Nashville Now* television show, but they'd also continued their history of meticulously looking for the right new guy to complete the band. Intentionally or not,

Dana sort of sewed the whole package together. As a personality, he was big, loud, sarcastic, and boisterously funny. But in the fabric of the group's sound, he was practically a stealth musician.

"With the bass in a band, nobody really hears it until it goes away," he laughs. "And then they go, 'What happened?' It's the same way it seems to be with my voice. It's there, [but] it kinda goes away, and it just blends really well."

Somebody needed to blend all the parts, because the Tennessee River Boys possessed a lot of distinctive elements. Marty Roe's enunciations put a hardline country edge on a lyric, Gene Johnson's knifelike tenor harmonies were easily recognized, Jimmy Olander's bent licks were immediately identifiable, and drummer Brian Prout used his traditional-pop and rock–R & B background for a drum sound that was both fatter and more sensitive than many of his contemporaries. Dan Truman's jazz and classical background gave the piano a different sound than the gospel–honky-tonk vibe in most country bands, and Gene's mandolin—well, there wasn't much of that instrument to be found on country radio in 1989.

A BEAUTIFUL BLEND

They worked diligently to knit the parts together before their January 23 appearance on Ralph Emery's TNN show. The guests that night included Charley Pride and Tanya Tucker, and they needed to sound as though they belonged.

"They rehearsed more for that TV show than I've ever rehearsed in my days," Dana says. "I mean, every single day—three, four, five hours a day, workin' on songs nobody ever heard of. They were convinced it needed to be original music."

Dana was used to working as a sideman for established artists, who had their own litany of familiar material to play, or in bar bands that played the hits. He'd typically copied other people's licks—now they needed him to come up with his own.

"Frankly," Gene says, "I think a lot of the time that we were sayin' we were gettin' together to practice, it wasn't so much for the rest of us as that we wanted to get Dana fittin' in and comfortable, [so] we could have the confidence in going out and playing somewhere without feeling that we might fall apart in the middle of it."

They did *Nashville Now* without a hitch, though their subsequent spring schedule kept changing. Top Billing booked live dates for the River Boys, but they inevitably disappeared. The band kept slaving away at material with the clothes dryer turned on for heat at their makeshift rehearsal space in Brian's dimly lit garage.

COLLEGE CONNECTIONS

Marty brought Monty Powell, his former David Lipscomb College buddy, to one of those rehearsals and introduced him around. Monty had hired Marty periodically to sing on jingles—the music that appears in TV and radio ads—but wanted to try his hand at producing commercial music. He was working with a couple of other prospective artists, Ron Hemby (who joined the 1990s group Buffalo Club) and Marcus Hummon (destined to cowrite Rascal Flatts's "Bless the Broken Road" and Sara Evans's "Born to Fly"), and he'd employed Jimmy O as a guitarist on some of those sessions.

Monty had installed a sixteen-track recording console in his basement near the Elm Hill Marina, past the airport on the east side of Nashville. After the band finished lengthy demo sessions, Marty would hang around with Monty and take a bass boat out on the lake and talk about their dreams of launching the band. Monty, in fact, had already formed a partnership with engineer Mike Clute and songwriters Tim DuBois and Van Stephenson, who were on the charts at that very moment with

Restless Heart's aptly titled "Big Dreams in a Small Town." Tim was talking with New York executive Clive Davis about starting a country division for Arista Records.

Clive saw potential in Nashville. Randy Travis had received plaques the previous year for two and three million sales of a couple of albums. He was a *traditional* singer, no less, and that was one of numerous signs to Clive that country had some potential for his label, which was already doing big business in the pop world with Whitney Houston, Exposé, and Milli Vanilli.

Monty played some of the River Boys' material for DuBois, who was intrigued by the demo but not completely sold.

"Mister," he told Marty, "I just don't think there's any room for any more bands in country music."

Country already had Alabama, Restless Heart, and Exile; vocal groups such as the Oak Ridge Boys, the Statler Brothers, and the Forester Sisters; and the California-based Southern Pacific and the Desert Rose Band. Plus, DuBois was already planning to sign Exile and maybe the established western-swing act Asleep at the Wheel. Instead of the River Boys, he said, he'd be much more interested in signing Marty as a solo act. Marty wasn't saying no to the offer, but he asked Tim to at least come and see the Tennessee River Boys live. He had invested six years in the group, had hung through some very rough times, and still believed in what they had to offer.

"I really think there's more uniqueness in the whole band and in the artistry of this band than I would bring myself," he told DuBois.

In fact, the River Boys were quite different from the other bands that were already established. Many of the groups used session musicians to record their albums, so apart from the harmonies, they didn't sound all that much different from the solo artists already dominating the genre. Southern Pacific and Desert Rose had West Coast roots that were entirely separate from Nashville-based acts. And Restless Heart and Exile, though they played their own instruments, used big, stacked harmonies to get a fuller sound. Each of the singers would double or triple their voices in the studio to make the records sound as if they had six or a dozen harmony guys instead of two or three.

The Tennessee River Boys had a "one guy, one part" philosophy, as Clute describes it. They played and sang the songs in the studio in a manner that allowed them to duplicate the sound on stage. Plus, with Gene's and Dana's roots, the River Boys had much more of a bluegrass vocal texture than the other bands, most of whom were derived from gospel roots or the Eagles.

JOINING THE ARISTA FAMILY

Once he was officially on board with Arista, DuBois consented to see them live, and the River Boys found a promoter willing to let them open at a George Jones show in Alabama during May 1989. The promoter paid them three hundred dollars—enough to rent a bus for the trip— and the guys had no more than twenty-five minutes to make their case.

1991 "We got that shot taken at Arista when we were there for an Alan Jackson party for 'Don't Rock The Jukebox' that featured George Jones." —Gene

Monty drove down to the date with DuBois and, no doubt, talked the band up during the trip and even in the middle of the show. But most of the River Boys kept their enthusiasm in check. They'd done showcases before, invariably amassing a pile of bills and receiving no offers. Plus, this wasn't for a label like RCA or Columbia or MCA—companies that had long track records of country music success with Ronnie Milsap, Willie Nelson, or George Strait. This was Arista, which had no artists officially signed and boasted an office with just two people: DuBois and Ramona Simmons.

"I didn't feel any pressure," Gene says. "It was like we were gonna do a show."

Jimmy, on the other hand, went to quite a bit of trouble for the date. His mother had made a Manuel-style, waist-length jacket with hand-painted black-and-white checks on the lapel, and Jimmy went on a quick diet to be as trim as possible.

"I was lookin' good in my new country music jacket with the big mullet and shaved sides," he laughs.

Most artists enlist as many friends as possible to pack the house for a showcase, hoping to sway label executives' minds as they evaluate an act's potential. Because this show was out of state, the River Boys had no buddies in the crowd and were essentially an unknown commodity. But they made a big impression. The audience, there to see a George Jones show, gave them a standing ovation. They'd clearly connected with the people—and they connected with DuBois as well.

After the show he came backstage and offered handshakes to all the guys. DuBois didn't give them a full-fledged deal on the spot, but he said he'd like to have them record three songs and see what they could do in the studio before he made a decision.

They were still showing some of the variety that had been a staple of the earlier River Boys incarnations. The bluegrass harmonies were solid, the playing was excellent, and the material was clearly country, though they still did the Dobie Gray song "If I Ever Needed You, I Need You Now," complete with a soaring '80s-power-ballad guitar solo from Jimmy O.

"I remember either Monty or Tim saying, 'Yeah, don't do that anymore,'" Jimmy says.

With that input and the cautious offer from Arista, the River Boys headed home on the bus with a mix of feelings.

"I came out of that goin', 'Hey, we've got a record deal!'" Marty says. "I'm a pretty optimistic guy. I'm always lookin' for the sunshine. Dana is like, '*Phhht*, I'll believe it when I see it.'"

Both of them were justified. Marty had pushed for the group instead of taking a solo deal, and DuBois had agreed with him that the band had something worth exploring. For his part, Dana recognized the precarious nature of the offer. Arista hadn't committed to a full album and could bail at any time. Making it even more tenuous, DuBois was insisting he would sign no more than eight or nine acts, and by the end of June, the label was committed to at least seven acts: Alan Jackson, Pam Tillis, Exile, Asleep at the Wheel, Lee Roy Parnell, Radney Foster, and Michelle Wright. Only one or two slots remained, and Arista was looking at a couple of other artists at the same time.

TIME OF SORROW—AN UNTIMELY DEATH

Making it all the more surreal, Gene's buddy, Keith Whitley, died in May—the same month they showcased for DuBois—from alcohol-related blood poisoning. The River Boys had a job the same day—at the Bluegrass Country Club, an odd coincidence since Gene and Keith had bonded in bluegrass.

Adding to the day's oddness, Gene's wife, June, was touched by Keith-related events several times that morning before she knew what had happened. First, Keith's ex-wife Kathy dropped by June's office at Masterfonics to pick something up and talked about him for about a half hour. Then

June received a phone call from the Davidson County medical examiner, Dr. Charles Harlan. He refused to acknowledge his identity, but she'd known him in her previous job and recognized his voice. He asked a bunch of questions about Keith—Did she know him? Was he famous?—then ended the call without explaining any of it.

Only afterward did she discover it was already on the radio: Keith had died.

June's encounters were "like *Twilight Zone* stuff," Gene recalls.

Gene had performed with Keith, shared hotel rooms, sung Lefty Frizzell songs together into the morning hours—he was understandably affected by Keith's passing.

"Me and Keith at the Birchmere. Hey, Afros were in style then." —Gene

"When you lose friends in this business like Keith, it is an eye-opener," Gene says. "It really makes you stop and look at the business and your place in it—where you're going and how to get there and what to do about it when you get there."

For the short term, Gene was mourning, though he remained fairly introspective about it, leaving his bandmates mostly to guess at what might be going on in his psyche.

"To see Gene affected like that, it was definitely a dark little period there," Dan says. "Gene's always mellow is the problem, but you could tell a definite difference in him. He was depressed."

ROMANCE FOR JIMMY

While Gene had lost a friend, Jimmy had made a new one. During one of the stops at Monty's basement to work on the band's sound, Marty and Robin had drug along Claudia Fontenot, who worked with Robin spritzing customers in the fragrance department at Castner Knott.

"I was actually set up by Marty Roe, who tries to deny it," says Jimmy, who had been quite happy living as a bachelor. "She's dressed in full-on Denver Bronco regalia—Bronco boxers with blue sweat pants—and she comes down in the studio. I thought she was pretty cute, and she thought I was cute, and I'm basically a relatively shy guy when it comes to women and stuff like that. So I didn't go for it until Marty, like two and a half weeks later—he does this sometimes when he gets really serious, he points his forehead at you—and he goes, 'You know, I reckon you oughta take her out.'"

"She's a hoot," Marty says. "We thought they would be a good match, and so far it's worked out. I don't claim any responsibility in case it falls apart—I've said that for the last seventeen or eighteen years."

Once they started dating, the Olander-Fontenot relationship developed quickly.

EXCRUCIATING WAIT

The signing process with Arista, however, dragged on for months. The label released its first country albums, by Alan Jackson and Exile, in February 1990. It was another two months before the River Boys officially signed the first contract—eleven months after their out-of-town showcase for DuBois.

The waiting was excruciating. Jimmy and Marty had signed their first songwriting deals with a publishing company, Warner Chappell, giving each of them an extra income of about fifteen thousand dollars a year. Arista advanced the band twenty-five thousand dollars. Split six ways, it wasn't particularly substantial, but at least they had no management taking an additional cut. Gene was doing cabinetry work for quick pay, and Dana and Brian did club gigs for measly amounts— fifty dollars here, thirty dollars there—while they all looked for songs to record.

Dan wasn't getting much work, but he had yet another mouth to feed. His third child, Casey Truman, happened along on June 16.

Dana was still working with Jeanne Pruett's band at the Grand Ole Opry, and they were leaving town for a gig one night when he ran out to a phone booth in the Shoney's parking lot in Goodlettsville to check in with one of the River Boys. It was then that he discovered they had indeed gotten their deal.

"I remember just screamin' as loud as I could scream in that phone booth," Dana says.

Jeanne bought a couple of apple pies the next night and had a little congratulations pie party. Then Dana went out with her band and performed somebody else's original licks from Jeanne's hit "Satin Sheets" one more time.

SONG QUEST

The River Boys had already started looking for material. Arista received plenty, too, but the band was given a lot of latitude in finding its own stuff.

"Our band almost outnumbered the employees at the label!" Dana laughs.

Marty and Brian struck gold one night at the Bluebird Café, a strip-mall listening room in Green Hills where songwriters performed their songs—familiar or not—to an attentive audience. Larry Cordle sang "Mama Don't Forget to Pray for Me," and the two River Boys introduced themselves and asked if they could cut it. They heard "Mirror Mirror" the same night, and both songs became future singles.

Dana and an Arista employee heard "Meet in the Middle," a song that had lain untouched for several years, while visiting publishers. Dan submitted another song for consideration called "Pretty Little Lady." DuBois gave that one a thumbs-up but insisted it needed to be personalized. The pretty little lady needed a name.

"I don't care whose name it is," he said. "It could be Norma Jean Riley. Anything!"

"Okay," Dan said. And the song became "Norma Jean Riley."

NAME QUEST

In addition to material, the River Boys were looking for a name. They needed to shed the Opryland image for good. And Tennessee River Boys had those bluegrass connotations. For a time they talked about Kilroy, then dumped it. They also toyed with the Mavericks—the name hadn't been used yet—but it morphed into the Twang Town Mavericks, which the band shortened to the T Town Mavericks. It kind of connected them to Nashville and carried an edgy connotation; the group was so sold on the idea that it had one thousand glossy publicity pictures made with that name. They liked it, and for a time they convinced themselves they could push Arista into accepting it.

Arista did not.

"So we went and found us a big old paper cutter in a school somewhere and chopped the bottom of them pictures off," Dana says. "We couldn't afford to buy any more. We just had to chop that name off and sell 'em anyway."

Mike Hollingsworth, the publisher who supplied them with "Meet in the Middle," told Dan he had a potential solution. Brian's former Heartbreak Mountain partner, Marty Raybon, had gone on to sing with a new group. That band had settled on Shenandoah as a name. One of the names they had passed on might have some value: Diamond Rio. Dan took that moniker back to his partners—though he didn't mention any of the Shenandoah connection. They particularly liked *Diamond* and came up with more than fifty ways to incorporate it into a name.

"It was really masculine," Dana says, "flashy, hard-hittin'."

Diamond Back lasted longer than any of the other fifty candidates, but they ultimately fell back on Diamond Rio, taken from the name of an old fire truck company.

Meanwhile, Marty Raybon and Shenandoah popped into town for Fan Fair during 1990. The group had built a nice little career for itself with three number-one singles the previous year—"The Church on Cumberland Road," "Sunday in the South," and "Two Dozen Roses"—and Marty wanted to meet up with Brian for drinks while the band was in town. Brian was instructed to come over to the Shoney's Inn on Demonbreun, at the edge of Music Row, and ask at the front desk for Marty Raybon of Diamond Rio.

Diamond Rio?

The name had not, it turned out, been completely abandoned: Marty Raybon's band was officially known as Shenandoah to the public, but they conducted business as Diamond Rio. It was the name the Shenandoah musicians had actually wanted to use, but their record company had rejected it. A beer or two into their conversation, Brian mentioned that his new band was actually considering Diamond Rio as their name. He was concerned that the Shenandoah guys might try to block them from using it. Ultimately Marty and his new partners gave their blessing to Brian's band. Diamond Rio hadn't worked out for them; Brian's band might as well have it.

In an ironic turn of events, in January 1991, Shenandoah filed for bankruptcy because of legal costs involving their own band name. Several other acts had already been labeled as Shenandoah. Diamond Rio, meanwhile, was free and clear to use—the name the Shenandoah members had wanted in the first place.

APPEARANCE UPGRADE VELCRO-STYLE

There were other issues to clear up with DuBois, too, typically with the six guys in a half circle of chairs around his desk at Arista. The band had told Dana when he joined that he needed to upgrade his appearance. They'd taken him to Ramon of California, an upscale salon at the Green Hills Mall, to clean him up. DuBois asked him to shed some of his 230 pounds.

Dana still had doubts that Arista was going to actually let them put an album out, and he didn't want to be the reason the deal fell apart. He went on a diet and started dropping the weight, but for extra measure, he bought an exercise belt with a Velcro strip to put around his waist before every meeting. It would make him look even thinner. But one of those conferences gave him away.

"I don't remember what the meeting was about," Dana says. "I went to cross my legs and stuff, and all of a sudden I hear *cccccccrick!* I heard that Velcro startin' to give way on my stomach in my shirt. I'm like, *Oh crap, man!* Every time I'd move—*cccccccrick*—I'd hear it again.

"Some of the guys knew what was goin' on and they was dyin' to laugh and didn't want to. Finally, we're sayin' good-bye, DuBois come over to me, shook my hand, patted me on the side, and said, 'Hey, man, you don't have to keep wearin' the corset.' I was completely busted by the record company president."

HEALTH CHALLENGES

"I Need to See Dr. Nixon."

There were, however, much bigger issues. Not the least of which was the health of the band. On August 9, a day before he turned forty-one, a construction accident put Gene's ability to play the mandolin in peril. While putting the finishing touches on some display cabinets for a computer store in Little Rock, he rushed a cut on a small piece of wood. The miter saw sucked the wood—and Gene's left thumb—into the ten-inch blade, carving out a huge chunk of flesh and bone lengthwise from the tip of the nail all the way past the first two joints.

Gene wrapped the thumb in a rag and headed to the emergency room. But before he left, he turned to his coworkers with one last request: "Take a look at the saw and see if there's any of my thumb that's left in there."

He suffered—in shock and in pain—through a frustrating delay at the ER. The nurse asked if he was there to see Dr. Nixon.

"I'm not from here," Gene told her. "I don't know your doctors."

She left, then came back a while later: "Are you here for Dr. Nixon?"

"I'm from out of town," he repeated. "I don't know any of the doctors."

What, he wondered, *is wrong with this woman?*

The nurse left yet again, only to return once more with the same question: "Are you here to see Dr. Nixon?"

"Yes," he finally said. "I need to see Dr. Nixon."

"Okay," she said. "I'll call him."

Dr. Nixon, Gene discovered, was the hand specialist. But hospital rules forbid the nurse from summoning a doctor who wasn't working the ER unless the patient requested him. She was, Gene recognized later, helping to save his thumb. Dr. Nixon sewed him up, but the damage was severe. He couldn't separate the ligaments from the muscle tissue, and Gene lost a huge amount of dexterity. For a couple of months he was uncertain about his future as a mandolin player.

June headed to Arkansas immediately, and as her husband healed in the hospital bed during the next three days, she pushed the morphine button whenever he expressed any kind of pain. As a result, those seventy-two hours were a blur to him.

For the guys in Diamond Rio—or the Tennessee River Boys, whatever name they were using now—there was a huge amount of shock. They didn't know at first if Gene would even be able to keep his thumb. His vocal abilities were the main reason they had picked him up, and he could still sing. The mandolin was something he brought to the band that was unique instrumentally, but they weren't yet sure if it would even be accepted once they put the album out. They took a huge breath and waited.

"[The mandolin] was something that was going to make us sound very different from anybody else," Jimmy says. "As you reflect on it, you go, *Wow, maybe that should have hit me more significantly than it did.* But it was just another thing—*big* thing—but it was actually more of a thing that your friend and your bandmate has a huge injury, than is this a career-ender? We didn't have a career. It's not like all of our hits were gonna be taken away from us."

In fact, they still had work to do. The band took off for Brazil later in the month on a tour with new artists Kevin Welch and Jann Browne, employing Robert Bolin as Gene's fill-in. During dinner at an open-air restaurant in Sao Paulo, a man strolled by the table, grabbed Robert's briefcase, and took off running. The entire entourage jumped up from the table and gave chase, mullets flying behind them.

Every block or so, they'd pass a group of Sao Paulo police casually watching. Somehow they told the cops who they were chasing and what he looked like. The police were unfazed, never started pursuit, but did get on the phone. A few blocks away, the burglar was apprehended in a weird, comedic moment.

Dana's Accident

The comedy didn't last, though. Upon their return Dana joined the disabled list. He went water-skiing with his family on September 6—exactly four weeks after Gene's accident. As they headed back at dusk, his wife, Lisa, tried to swing the boat back to pick Dana up in the middle of the lake. The carburetor got stuck; she hit the gas a couple of times and the engine engaged once again. But it lurched forward at breakneck speed. She had little time to maneuver and at the last second was barely able to swing a sharp left and avoid running directly over her husband.

But the back end of the boat swung over him, and the propeller sliced both of Dana's legs. In the dark, he couldn't tell what had happened. He just knew it hurt and that he needed to grab for his leg in case it had been completely severed.

"It felt like somebody took a sledgehammer and hit my knee," he says. "I reached down to grab my leg, to see if it was there, and my hand got real hot. Keep in mind, I'm underwater. My hand got real hot, and I went, *Oh, I think I'm in my leg.*"

Part of his left femur, the strongest bone in the body, had sheared off and was tucked inside the mangled part of his leg. The family lifted Dana out of the water, packed his legs in ice, then took him to the hospital for emergency surgery. Two screws were inserted permanently into the left leg to rejoin the femur. He awoke in a Cookeville hospital to find five staples in his right knee and nineteen in his left, with an automated motion machine forcing gradual movement of his legs to keep the muscles from deteriorating. The doctors weren't completely convinced he'd be able to walk again.

The band had a gig to do on the Atlantic coast, so on the way out of Nashville the guys swung by Cookeville to see Dana. Somehow they were relieved. It was a serious injury, and the contraption that kept his legs moving was completely strange. But they could tell he'd recover well. Even if he couldn't walk, he could sit on a stool and still play and sing. He was somehow going to be okay.

Brian Helgos took Dana's place on that trip. Paul Gregg, of Restless Heart, would fill in on a couple of other concert runs.

Jimmy's Battle

Still, there was more bad news on the way. Jimmy had developed an upper respiratory problem. He had a lemon-sized mass in his chest that pressed against his esophagus. It affected his breathing and his ability to swallow, and he and Claudia—who had moved in with Jimmy—lost sleep as he endured severe night sweats.

"I wasn't a pajamas guy, but I had become a pajamas guy just because of the sopping effect," he says. "I had to change pajamas, and we had to remake the bed because I would soak the bed—for about six weeks to two months, every night: soak the bed, get up change the sheets, change the pajamas, feel like crap, there's a tumor in your chest, I go back for more blood work and more tests every other day, it's never diagnosed, we cruise on 'til my symptoms subside."

"He had this weird cough that would come up," Dana notes. "It was really bizarre, and if you turn [the volume] way up on the outro of 'They Don't Make Hearts Like They Used To' on the first record, you can hear Jimmy wheezing. It's just guitar being played there, [so] you can hear Jimmy wheezing a little bit. We were cuttin' [music despite] all that stuff."

It seemed as if Diamond Rio was plagued. Dana was confined to the bed in his living room, recuperating in front of bad daytime television for at least six weeks. Gene had to wait two months to start rehabbing his thumb, beginning to gingerly play the mandolin in October with a massive bandage restricting his movement. And Jimmy, age twenty-nine, was breathing like a geriatric patient. The band began to doubt if it would ever get the first album done. DuBois started joking that they should lock themselves in a closet until they got it finished.

"Not bein' one of those guys," Dan says, "I just remember goin', *Is this bad karma? Or is this just somethin' that happened?*"

Bringing It Back Together

By December, Gene had regained enough use of his thumb to warrant a return to the recording studio to overdub mandolin parts. The joint that connects the thumb to the hand, close to the wrist, was still completely flexible; but the thumb's two outer joints barely moved at all. As a result, he was unable to wrap the thumb over the neck of the mandolin, changing his grip and the force with which he moved the other four fingers. Gene had to run through a series of stretching exercises before he played—and does so to this day—but some of the hot-shot licks he once ripped through with ease were no longer available to him.

"If you go back and listen to how I played with David Bromberg to how I play now, I'm more tasteful now," he says. "I definitely had a lot more speed, and the distance from my head to my fingers was closer."

During the overdub sessions, Gene was a "trooper," Clute says. Still, Gene threatened to walk away—though not because of his injury or the mandolin. Monty made an offhand remark to Gene about bringing Marty back in to overdub the high vocal harmonies—the part that Gene had fought for when he first joined the band. Marty would, in effect, end up singing with himself on the recordings, while Gene and Dana would do the harmony parts on the road. It's the way Monty had done it when he recorded jingles with Marty and it made perfect sense to him.

Gene didn't take Monty's comment as an insult, but he didn't take it in stride either. "I said, 'No, Monty, this is a deal-breaker to me. I've got to sing on the records or I'm not gonna go out and sing on the road.' I just felt that I had to stand up and fight for this, and if it meant that I left the band, well, we weren't makin' any money with this yet. It was complete speculation, and I was willing to walk."

Neither Gene nor Monty consulted with the other band members. Monty might have talked about it with DuBois. Either way, Gene ended up layering those distinctive, in-your-face harmonies over Marty's lead vocals on the album.

"It was the right thing to do," Jimmy says. "Dana blends and he's bluegrassy, but Gene to me is the distinctive element of the harmonies for Diamond Rio. If Marty sang the harmonies with himself, it would just sound like the Carpenters, which is all smoothy and blendy and nondescript."

"The thing that stamps our trio," says Dana the blender, "is Gene's voice."

THE REAL DEAL

Peter Nash Photographer

Released 1991

The album was mixed and mastered at Masterfonics—appropriate, since June still worked there. Arista invited Diamond Rio to its first gold record party to celebrate Alan Jackson's *Here in the Real World*—demonstrating that it was indeed a real record label and making the guys feel part of a team, even if the rest of the world didn't know them yet. The label set February 6 as the release date for the first single, "Meet in the Middle."

First Photo Shoot: 17 Hours

There was plenty to do in the meantime. The first photo shoot was an ordeal—much more work than they expected just to take some pictures. They had to decide on a photographer, a location, clothing—then the photographer made remarks throughout the session about how frustrated he was trying to fit six people into a picture and still have it seem creative.

They visited Georgia to shoot their first music video, showing up on location at 10:00 AM, only to sit around the set—which hadn't been prepped—until almost 7:00 PM. Making matters worse, Dana had the flu, causing him to make periodic bathroom visits. And then news of the day brought everyone to a standstill: the U.S. had just begun bombing Iraq. They turned on the tube and watched the surreal coverage for a bit, then went back to work until 3:00 AM—a seventeen-hour day for a three-minute sales piece.

"We quickly learned that that was not the way it was supposed to go," Dana says. "But buddy, that was a painful, painful ordeal right there."

The Final "Blue Hair Tour"

The band had one more series of subscription concerts—the "Blue Hair Tour," they liked to call it—to complete as the Tennessee River Boys. Arista footed the bill for a bus, allowing them to bid a farewell to the bread truck they'd used for the last year or so. In return, they agreed to visit radio stations along the way and promote "Meet in the Middle."

Marty and Robin had a baby due any day, so they induced labor February 8 to make sure Marty had time with his newborn before he hit the road. They brought Isabella home two days later, then Marty joined the guys at TNN the next morning for the premiere of their video. From there they hit the road, and Marty wouldn't see Izzy for another two weeks.

It was a weird transition for the entire band. They visited radio stations in the morning as Diamond Rio to promote the single, had lunch with radio personalities and programmers who had the power to either

Dr. Rubel Shelly, Isabella, Robin, Marty

play or snub their music, then performed on stage at night as the Tennessee River Boys, where they announced during the show that they had changed their name.

The guys were worn out, and Marty in particular was torn—happy with their new career opportunity but frustrated, missing his daughter's first days of life. It was even worse for Robin, who came out to see the band perform in Indiana. Marty mentioned from the stage that his wife was in the audience. Robin overheard a couple of girls muttering that she was the "luckiest woman in the world." She felt like the loneliest.

"Those first few years, to be honest with you, were not easy for her," Marty says. "I was eat up with what I was doin', and when I came home, I hadn't adjusted to that kind of lifestyle. I'd come home, I didn't wanna do anything, I wouldn't help . . . out on the road, everybody's waitin' on you hand and foot. We struggled for a little while in '92 and '93."

Dana, meanwhile, was in healing mode. He'd followed the doctor's orders to the letter and reclaimed the ability to walk. But he wasn't exactly running yet.

"For probably I'd say five years, there's many times that I would trip goin' up on stage," he says. "It's all because that tendon was shorter now, where they cut it, and I would raise my leg to go up a step. In actuality, [the leg] didn't pick up [as far as I thought], because that tendon is different now, so I would trip and fall. Then I got to where I was overcompensatin', tryin' to go up steps and stuff. I didn't wanna fall and bust my guitar all to pieces, but I went through several years where I had to work on not trippin' and fallin'."

Breaking Records with "Meet in the Middle"

Once the "Blue Hair" jaunt was over, the Tennessee River Boys/ Diamond Rio suddenly found themselves without any real tour schedule for a couple of months. They also found themselves with a hit on their hands—a bigger hit than just about anyone had expected. "Meet in the Middle"—with its little signature guitar lick, chugging bass-and-drum interplay, and tight harmonies—climbed all the way to Number One in *Billboard* and stayed there for two weeks. It was the first time in the history of the chart, then forty-seven years old, that a group had gone to the top with its debut single.

Gene drove over to Jimmy's house in Inglewood, where they broke open a bottle of wine and rewrote "The Ballad of Jed Clampett," to salute the label's promotion team. They then called Allen Butler, head of the department, to sing him the new lyrics.

But they were, once again, barely working.

"'Meet in the Middle' seemed to catch everybody by surprise," Gene says. "I think we might have been the only ones that believed it would go number one. When it did, then nobody was ready. Things should've been happening, and they weren't. But that's all hindsight."

The band gave its first official concert as Diamond Rio on May 4, 1991, part of a free radio station promotion at a parking lot in Columbus, Ohio, where they shared the bill with Wild Rose.

It was an inauspicious debut. Wild Rose, the all-female band, gave a great opening set. Rio followed, and they could see the other band—including Brian's wife, Nancy—in the crowd, which was fairly sparse. They played under a canvas cover, the sound was loud and unruly, and so was Marty's voice. He had severe pitch problems, and the guys could see it in the faces of the Wild Rose musicians, who grimaced at times as if they were being punched.

"Then we have to do it all over again, two shows," Jimmy recalls. "Dana and I get off stage, go into the back lounge of the bus, sittin' there, didn't say anything. I think I might've been the first one to speak, and I said, 'I'm not leavin' here. I'm not goin' out. This is too embarrassing.'"

They did, of course, go back for the second show. It was part of the job.

A similar episode occurred when Diamond Rio joined Pam Tillis at Legislative Plaza in Montgomery, Alabama. She was on the money, while Marty struggled with pitch.

"At that point," Jimmy says, "I went, 'Okay, this is all gonna just quit. This is all gonna go away.'"

Fan Fair and "Conductor" Billy Dean

In June the group played to its first huge audience as Diamond Rio during the annual Fan Fair celebration in Nashville. They signed autographs in triple-digit heat at an exhibit booth at the fairgrounds. Billy Dean, who'd played for a brief period in a club band with Brian, had the booth right next to them. The fans were crowded around, trying to get their first real glimpse of Diamond Rio, when someone started singing "Meet in the Middle." It became a mass chorus of fans—"I'd start walkin' your way / You'd start walkin' mine"—while Billy did a silly imitation of a conductor as the Rio guys frantically signed autographs. For Brian, who'd collected autographs at Fan Fair during '83, it was a huge role reversal.

"There I was, eight years later, bein' one of those people that we used to come and follow around and want one of their autographs," he says. "It was one of those cool moments."

Fan Fair 1991, Tennessee Fairgrounds. *Left to right*: Dana, Gene, Jimmy, Marty, Dan, Brian. "It was always blistering hot . . . the fans would wait for hours with barely a breeze to meet their favorite country artists." —Brian

The Fan Fair performance, in front of fifteen thousand people, had them on the same bill as the rest of the Arista roster, including Rob Crosby, Pam Tillis, and Brooks & Dunn, who'd just released their first single. Diamond Rio had the last slot before Alan Jackson, thanks in part to their recent trip to number one. Just before they hit the stage, they had another meeting with the company president.

"Tim DuBois pulls us all together," Brian says, "and he puts his arms around us, huddles us up, and says, 'Misters, don't [mess] this up.'"

The show went without a hitch, and the folks were emphatic in their appreciation for "Meet in the Middle," but the band was already taking steps to shore up those potential sound issues. Instead of relying on stage monitors, they ordered ear molds that were custom-designed to fit each musician. The sound system was a new technology that helped control an unpredictable situation. The monitors cost eleven thousand dollars per player—a whopping sixty-six thousand dollars for six guys who were just starting to get five-hundred-dollar checks every week—but it seemed to solve any issues they had in hearing themselves as they moved from venue to venue.

"It was," Jimmy says, "the best money I've ever spent in my life."

The Road

The schedule might have been lean at the outset, but Diamond Rio soon took a barrage of dates. It had been seven years since Marty had joined the Tennessee River Boys, and after the long struggle, they all wanted to take advantage of the opportunities. Not surprisingly, their itinerary soon swung from slow to overloaded.

"I'd been on the road for fourteen or fifteen years when I meet these guys—sixteen years, I guess," Gene says. "So I'd already traveled the entire country playin' music. I was ready—let's get out there and make some money! They got over the top with it. I'm goin', 'We gotta have a week off, take a little time here and there.' I was in a completely different place. I had teenage kids, and Marty only had a baby; Dan had kids, but they were real small, and I was more or less wanting to be home a little more at some points during those early years when we just seemed to run and run and run."

The dates were often at clubs and small theaters, where the audience was close. They'd heard plenty of the "sex, drugs, and rock 'n' roll" stories from other artists, but they were stunned at the volume and the relentlessness of it all.

"You hear 'Meet in the Middle,' it doesn't make me wanna take my shirt off," Dana laughs. "But there for a while, there was a lot of girls out there that felt like they needed to take their shirts off when they heard that song. It didn't bother me a bit, I tell you."

But there were situations where it got extremely uncomfortable. In the autograph lines after the shows, women wanted signatures on their behinds, on their front pockets, even on their breasts—and they didn't mind lifting their shirts in public to get inked. Marty and Dana initially refused, but Gene signed as quickly as possible and moved them along.

"You can argue about it," Gene says, "but they're gonna stand there a lot longer."

"I signed so many boobs, which I know all these artists do, but there's some that stand out," Dana adds. "I remember one girl that came up to me *with her husband* and wanted me to sign her boobs, and I didn't have a pen, so he let me borrow his. He said, 'Aw, you can keep it.' I'm like, *Is this okay?*—as I'm dotting the 'i'!"

Most of the time the women were trying to find a way to get close to the guys in the band. At concert halls they were known to throw bras on stage (the Diamond Rio record is an eighteen-bra night at the Cal State Expo in Sacramento) and then appear at the side door later, claiming they needed to retrieve their lingerie. But it wasn't just fans who played the game. Often in that first year, the band would retire to the bus at the end of the night only to find a stripper—or two—left for their "pleasure" by a promoter, a club owner, or somebody who thought they were doing them a favor.

One night someone affiliated with a show appeared at the bus with a bag of cocaine. Sending a very clear message, they turned him away at the door.

"People think, *Well, they're a band, so we really need to give 'em something they'll remember us by,*" Dan says. "Either drugs or strippers."

In perhaps their biggest test, they were introduced to a whole group of strippers when they performed in Pensacola. A crew member promised to bring the guys by a club on the way out of town, and the owner opened the doors to give the band a private show. The women started into their routine, the clothes began coming off, and they used Diamond Rio as a soundtrack, stripping to "Mama Don't Forget to Pray for Me." In short order, the chorus hit home: "No, I ain't forgot how I was raised / But I'm livin' way too fast—"

The guys looked at each other, winced in embarrassment, and headed to the door. It was an eye-opening irony. They had hoped their music would have a positive effect on the world at large, but they realized the world outside could instead have a very negative effect on the way they conducted their business.

"Here's these all-American guys who have the Christian ideal of girls from Christian homes," Dan looks back. "It becomes so in-your-face and so available, and how you handle it—well, we didn't handle it perfectly, but we eventually handled it."

The band instigated a no-women-on-the-bus rule. It gave them some insulation from the outside world, a stable place to go to stay focused in cities away from home where it was tough to tell what people wanted from them—and why they wanted it.

Music That Makes a Difference

"Mama Don't Forget to Pray for Me," released on the heels of "Mirror Mirror" in the fall of '91, helped underscore their purpose—not only because of the Pensacola incident but also because it brought home their desire to make a difference in the lives of the people who heard them.

"We were gettin' lots of fan mail and letters at that point of time, and I remember one in particular from some girl that had run away from home and had been gone for six months or something and called home because of that song," Gene says, his eyes watering. "Man, it touches you. We already didn't wanna do the drinkin' songs and stuff, but that really drove it home. If you're gonna touch someone, touch them with something that's positive. Don't lead 'em off [to] the wrong place. Hit 'em with something that makes you do something right."

Gene was particularly susceptible to the sentiment of "Mama Don't Forget to Pray for Me." His father, Vern, was suffering from severe, Parkinson's-related dementia. Vern never really got to experience any of Diamond Rio's success; he died within a year after "Mama Don't Forget" was released.

Meanwhile, the no-women-on-the-bus rule helped reduce the number of family issues that could have interfered with the band's business.

"If we start bringin' our women on here, then all of a sudden you got twelve people on the bus," Dana says. "Not only is it crowded, but now all of a sudden there's six more opinions, and let's face it, have you ever seen six women that can get along for very long? We set this flat-out rule, and [now] we don't have that worry. I've seen many a band fall apart because somebody got mad from what somebody else's wife said to another wife and that wife told so and so and blah-dee-dah-dah-dah. So we just kinda nixed that from the beginning. I know it was a very wise decision at that time and still is."

AWARD TIME!

The band attended the Nashville-based Country Music Association Awards for the first time in the fall of '91, then picked up its first nominations at the Los Angeles–based Academy of Country Music Awards in

Left to right: Ted Hacker (International Artist Mgmt/ manager), Marty, Dana, Gene, Dan, Brian, Anita Hogin (International Artist Mgmt), Jimmy. "Our debut album was certified gold . . . such a small label and the fact that we were having this kind of success was truly remarkable for everyone." —Brian

April '92, just a month after "Norma Jean Riley" waltzed onto the national charts. Their debut album had just gone gold a month before. But they were caught off guard when they took home a prize from the ACMs: Top Vocal Group, given to them over Alabama, the Kentucky HeadHunters, Highway 101, and Marty Raybon and Shenandoah.

"I did not think we would win that," Marty Roe says, recalling the trip to the podium, "so I was scared to death."

He gave the acceptance speech and—as artists typically do—thanked God.

"I try not to thank God just for the success," he explains. "When I do that, I try to thank God just for the gift of doing this thing. I don't think God really cares whether I win an award or not. I think He cares about how I handle whatever award I win."

Marty had no idea how soon he would be tested. After the ACM had handed out the Top Group award, it still had a trophy to present for Top New Vocal Duet or Group. Just minutes before, Marty had been scared to accept one award; now he was convinced they were winning another.

"I got that [Vocal Group] trophy in my hand," he remembers, "and I'm goin', *We're two-fisted tonight, baby.* I'm thinkin' we won the Group of the Year, we're probably gonna win New Group, you know. *Yeah, we're two-fisted!*"

Back in their seats, he started giving the other guys directions about the best route to the stage.

"I was cocky as all get out, man."

That is, until the award went to Brooks & Dunn.

"From 'No way, we're not gonna get anything this year' to 'We're two-fisted' to 'We're goin' this way,' you talk about a change in attitude," Marty says while shaking his head. "The good Lord set me right down immediately, 'Nope, this is all you get tonight.'"

Three days later, the evening—and its trophies—seemed to be mostly hype to Dana, who figured no one would remember who won anyway.

Courtesy of the Academy of Country Music

1992 ACM Awards

© Beth Gwinn Courtesy of Country Music Association, Inc.

1992 CMA Awards. *Left to right*: **Brian, Dan, Gene, Dana, Marty, Jimmy.**

Jimmy didn't need three days. Competitive since his early years in go-carting and sailing in California, he was surprisingly despondent by the time he got back to his room.

"I'm sitting on the end of the hotel bed, and I'm in what at the time I thought was really stylish—a jacket and blue jeans—and I looked at that award and just got depressed," he says. "*Is this really it?* The thing that I was so looking forward to and was so hard to get—here it is, and it felt like 'that's over.' Not like my career's over, but I been workin' so hard and doin' all this stuff, and I got [the award], and just sitting there, bummed out."

"It's the journey, and not the destination," he continues. "In our awards-show winning, I figured that one out."

There was plenty of figuring to do in the years that followed. They repeated the next year at the ACMs, and they won the CMA Vocal Group honors in '92, '93, and '94. The trophy went the next two years to the Mavericks—ironic, since Diamond Rio had wanted to be the T Town Mavericks—and the CMA gave Rio one more victory in 1997.

Photo courtesy of Academy of Country Music

1993 ACM Top Vocal Group. *Left to right*: Brian, Dan, Marty, Dana, Jimmy, and Gene.

"The '97 CMA is probably the one that I ended up savoring the most," Marty reflects. "And I definitely came to peace with the idea that this could be the last time. I thought we'd already had it, but this could definitely be the last time we get one of those, unless somethin' really weird happens. That's just kind of how that works. And Randy Owen, he told me that long ago—Alabama had won obviously before us—and he said at a certain point they gave them Artist of the Decade at the ACMs, and he goes, 'Now this right here, guys, is their way of saying you're done.'"

DIAMOND RIO'S VOICE TO THE MEDIA

At the time of their first ACM win, Diamond Rio had other pressing things to consider. Among them was how best to represent the band. They'd attempted the first time out to do mass interviews, sometimes with all six band members talking to journalists. The stories were invariably disappointing—a journalist can cover a lot more ground in twenty or thirty minutes with one person than with six people in the same amount of time. Their management and publicists were pushing to have one group member—Marty, preferably, since he was the lead singer and conveyed the lyrics—give the band a more focused identity in the media.

"Some guys had mixed feelings about it," Dan says. "I sure did. I didn't wanna do all the interviews. I really didn't wanna do one-sixth of them. And yet you hear this and you go, *Is that really right?* You have a really strong band here—strong musicians and strong personalities. Is that gonna work for us?"

They hashed it out in a Florida hotel. Brian, who'd figured out how important a lead singer was when he was with Heartbreak Mountain, had nevertheless wanted to step forward in the media. He felt slighted by the decision.

"It was important to me that I got recognized," he says. "You know, *I'm the drummer in the band, and I should have as big a voice, and I can do an interview better than Marty Roe.*"

Ultimately, they decided to give Marty half the interviews and spread the other half among the remaining five members.

"To be quite honest with you, I didn't necessarily wanna do it all that much," Marty says. "That just became my job."

"They had to win him over and say, 'You need to be more aggressive and take the lead,'" Dan says. "And then when that happened, it wasn't just interviews; it was other things. It was just Marty, Marty, Marty. It could get a little weird, 'cause he was doin' all the work and we were sitting around. And then at times he would be a little put out 'cause he was doin' everything."

SUCCESS IS A HARD ACT TO FOLLOW

Jeff Frazier

The entire band suffered from overwork when it came time to do the second album. In classic music-business fashion, the label wanted to quickly follow up *Diamond Rio* with another CD after the first yielded five Top 10 hits. But where they'd been in dire need of work just a year

© Beth Gwinn

Fan Fair 1993. Presented with Diamond Rio's first-ever platinum award.

© Beth Gwinn

1993. The Platinum party for our first album. *Left to right:* Monty Powell (co-producer), Gene, Dana, Jimmy, Tim DuBois (Arista president, co-producer), Brian, Marty, Dan, Ted Hacker (manager, International Artist Mgmt).

or two before, the band was now in huge demand and had a difficult time fitting recording sessions into the schedule.

There was also plenty of analysis about why the first album worked. A couple of the singles from the first album—particularly "Mirror Mirror" and "Norma Jean Riley"—had a tinge of a novelty feel to them. And as they shoehorned the sophomore project into their itinerary, Billy Ray Cyrus exploded with "Achy Breaky Heart." Publicly, Music Row attacked that song for its simplicity. Privately, record labels—and a lot of artists—wanted the kind of financial success that goes with an album that sells nine million copies, as did Billy Ray's *Some Gave All.*

"[At the time] I think we need to just be doin' novelty stuff," Jimmy says. "I got a couple of cuts on that record. One of 'em is 'This Romeo Ain't Got Julie Yet'—by far not the best song Eric Silver and I [have] ever written together, by far not my favorite Diamond Rio recording—but that's at the time when I'm thinkin', *Oh, this is easy. Let's write this. It's kinda cute.*"

Two of the four singles from their second album, *Close to the Edge*—"Romeo" and "Oh Me, Oh My, Sweet Baby"—were silly. As singles, they were the album's sales pieces, and they made the project appear rather shallow.

Jeff Frazier

Released in 1992

"When everybody that's around you is tellin' you, 'Man, that's awesome, fantastic,' it makes it even more difficult," Dana notes. "Somebody tells you it's awesome, that's all you need, baby."

The band recalibrated as it headed toward its third album, *Love a Little Stronger.* They would still put out music with lighthearted messages—"Bubba

Hyde" and "Unbelievable," both issued later in the decade, weren't intended to make people cry—but Diamond Rio was never as susceptible to the easy road again. As they worked on *Love a Little Stronger*, Marty thought it might be appropriate to pay a nod to some of their influences on occasion by doing a cover song. In particular, he suggested remaking something by the Eagles, who had clearly had a huge impact on the state of country music in the '90s.

Released in 1994

"What they did lends itself to us very well," Marty says. "I even brought up 'Lyin' Eyes'—'That's a country song, we should do something like that on this next project.' I was talkin' to Tim DuBois about it. He's like, 'No, I don't think you guys need to be doin' copy stuff yet.' He just wasn't into it at all."

Benefit Projects

Don Henley, one of the Eagles' founders, contacted Diamond Rio's management firm, International Artist Management, about an album he was putting together that would benefit the Walden Woods Project, created in 1990 to preserve land near the home of nineteenth-century author Henry David Thoreau.

Don had recognized the same thing Marty had. The Eagles, who'd broken up more than a decade earlier, had left a huge mark on country music, and Don was assembling a series of Eagles covers. He asked Diamond Rio to donate its portion of the proceeds to Walden Woods, and it was easy to say yes. Don Henley had asked them personally—heck, they were flattered he even knew who they were.

They did the entire six-and-a-half-minute version of "Lyin' Eyes"—the song DuBois had nixed—with Marty giving it a lonesome read and Jimmy throwing in his patented bender licks. *Common Thread: The Songs of the Eagles* had full-circle significance for them. Not only had most of the band played Eagles songs in the clubs on the way up, the piano parts on the original 1975 version had been played by Jim Ed Norman, the same Warner Bros. executive who had given the Tennessee River Boys advice just a few years earlier.

The album—which also featured Vince Gill, Trisha Yearwood, Travis Tritt, and Clint Black, among others—became a source of controversy shortly after its release. While the artists gave away their royalties—probably more than three hundred thousand dollars per artist—Giant Records, which issued it, was keeping its share and using the money to compete against the labels that had allowed their artists to participate. A number of Nashville executives were furious, including DuBois, and Don circled the wagons to protect the money for his charity.

He called the artists one by one to lobby for their continued support and took Diamond Rio to lunch at Merchant's, a well-regarded restaurant in downtown Nashville. A couple of artists rescinded their contributions to Walden, but Diamond Rio was more than happy to let Henley's organization keep their proceeds.

"It made us feel like we'd made it in a way, the idea that Don Henley'd be talkin' to us," Gene says.

The project won the CMA's Album of the Year award in 1994, the same year that it initiated the reformation of the Eagles.

It also marked the first of several tribute albums that Diamond Rio took part in. They covered "Ten Feet Away" in honor of Gene's late friend on *Keith Whitley: A Tribute Album*. And they teamed up with Arista label mates Lee Roy Parnell and Steve Wariner for "Workin' Man Blues" on *Mama's Hungry Eyes: A Tribute to Merle Haggard*, with money from that project benefiting Second Harvest food banks.

They called their assembly Jed Zeppelin—Brian had lobbied, unsuccessfully, for Merle Jam—and got a CMA nomination in the process. Even better, they got to perform on the CMA Awards to set up Merle Haggard's induction into the Country Music Hall of Fame.

"I got hung by my hero there," Marty says, laughing. "After we've played 'Workin' Man Blues,' I think he shakes hands with Vince Gill, Emmylou Harris was on stage and Marty Stuart; anyhow, he shakes hands with them, and I stick my hand out to shake hands and he just turns—bloop—right on by me. Blew me off. Goes to the mic. And it's right on camera. Dana or somebody taped it, and they run it back and forth, back and forth on the bus."

MORE LIFE CHALLENGES

Brian and Nancy Prout bit the dust. Marty and Robin had a second daughter, Sarah, in November 1994; Dan and Wendee added a daughter, McKenzie, in 1995; and Dana and Lisa had their only son, Jacob, the following year.

March 1997. "Me and Marvin trying to show Jacob a G chord but for some reason he was more interested in the strings. Go figure at 10 months old!" —Dana

Big sister Izzy, baby Sarah, and Dad

Big brothers Chad, Ben, and Casey with baby sister McKenzie

By that point, Jimmy had gone through a life-changing recurrence of the tumor and night sweats that had plagued him when Diamond Rio was recording its debut album. This time around was even more dramatic. His esophagus was restricted once again—this time so severely that he refused to eat when he was alone.

188

"We're at gigs, I've got this flarin' up, there's a deli tray—pretty standard—I want a little piece of turkey," he says. "I can remember going, *I don't need to have anything to eat unless somebody's around, in case I choke.*"

"Hanging from the top wing of an upside-down Pitts biplane over Quincy, Illinois." —Jimmy

Jimmy underwent batteries of tests without getting a diagnosis. Doctors considered AIDS. Even though he knew it was remote, the test scared Jimmy. He was, fortunately, HIV-negative. One doctor suggested that a foreign object—maybe a chicken bone—had been lodged in his throat and his body had walled it off as a defense mechanism, creating the tumor. That, too, was ruled out. Finally he was sent to an oncologist who put him under a light anesthetic that left him awake while the doctor ran a tube down his nasal passage. The doctor's conversation during the procedure created a huge amount of fear. Jimmy was afraid he had cancer.

In considering his life—and the possibility that he might lose it—he realized he'd left some things undone. His relationship with his parents had deteriorated, he'd never gone skydiving, he hadn't learned to play the Dixie Dregs's "Pride O' the Farm," and he'd never actually married Claudia.

Ultimately the tumor was never diagnosed. One doctor treated it like

© Libba Gillum Photographer

tuberculosis and crossed his fingers that it would go away. And the tumor has, according to appearances, vanished. In the aftermath of his cancer scare, he went skydiving (Jimmy's gone on to skydive more than seven hundred times), he learned the Dregs's song, and it came time to tie the knot. With eleven days' notice, he and Claudia got married October 30, 1995, providing a sweet little storyline as the *Love a Little Stronger* album went platinum.

© Brian Erler—www.aerialartists.com

"Skydiving with Space Shuttle Discovery on its final mission to Mir Space Station. The boots . . . not my idea. Imagine—after your parachute opens—looking down for a place to land and you see a pair of size 14 cowboy boots!" —Jimmy

NEW CHAPTERS

Diamond Rio continued to write new chapters, and they did it while conveniently averting internal dramas. Their *IV* album ushered in Mike Clute as a co-producer with the band. *IV* became the first country release recorded entirely on a digital console. The first single, "Walkin' Away," could've easily applied to their professional relationship—"We've still got it good no matter how bad it gets"—while their quirky, conspiracy-theory–themed "It's All in Your Head" enlisted Martin Sheen for the video.

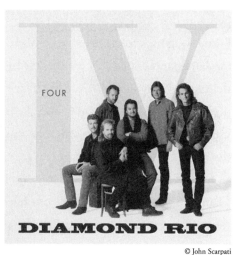

© John Scarpati

Released 1996

They netted another number-one single with 1997's "How Your Love Makes Me Feel"—often referred to as "the ice cream song"—added along with the Bryan White–penned "Imagine That" to pad their first *Greatest Hits* album.

Released 1997

Despite six years on the radio and their frequent trips to the awards podium, it was the first time Gene really felt they'd made it.

The *Hits* album "kind of caught us all by surprise," he says. "'What? We've had enough for a greatest-hits album?' That was kind of a little reassuring. *I guess we have been here a while, haven't we?* It made it seem like that."

191

Grand Ole Opry

Putting an exclamation point to it all was their 1998 induction into the Grand Ole Opry. The Tennessee River Boys had, after all, gotten their start at Opryland, built around the Opry. Dan, Jimmy, and Marty had all performed at the park; Brian had spent significant time with Opry legend Porter Wagoner when his ex-wife Nancy was a member of Porter's backing band; and Dana—whose uncles, the Osborne Brothers, had been on the Opry roster since 1964—had played as a backup musician for Opry members Jimmy C. Newman and Jeanne Pruett. Gene had dialed in the Opry back in Sugar Grove when he was a kid trying to find bluegrass on the radio.

Little Jimmy Dickens officially inducted them on April 18, making Diamond Rio the first band to join the Opry in fourteen years. In return the guys have made a commitment to playing on the show regularly.

© 2009 Grand Ole Opry Archives. Photo by Donnie Beauchamp.

April 18, 1998. "It meant an awful lot to the entire band, but especially to Dana given his ties to the Opry through his uncles, the Osborne Brothers. Little Jimmy Dickens inducted us into the Opry." —Brian

"There's a little bit of insecurity," Jimmy admits, "that [people will] find out I can't actually do this. Now I'm an Opry member, but I still

© 2009 Grand Ole Opry Archives. Photo by Donnie Beauchamp.

© 2009 Grand Ole Opry Archives. Photo by Chris Hollo.

10th Anniversary Photo. *Left to right*: Brian, Gene, Dana, Ted Greene (Manager/Modern Mgmt), Dan, Jimmy, Mike Clute (producer), Marty.

have some of those adolescent insecurities. I'm gonna be found out. But I love the Opry. I love takin' friends out to it. I love when Claudia tells the seventy-first member of the Grand Ole Opry to please take out the

© 2009 Grand Ole Opry Archives. Photo by Chris Hollo.

April 18, 2008. "It was hard to believe it had already been ten years and it still means just as much to us in our career. There is no greater honor in this industry." *Left to right*: Dan, Jimmy, Gene, Pete Fisher (GM of Grand Ole Opry), Dana, Bill Anderson, Marty.

trash. That's a quote: 'Will the seventy-first member of the Grand Ole Opry please take the trash out?' 'Yes, honey.'"

Tabloid Attention

Within six months of their Opry membership, the band—or, more specifically, Brian—became a regular attraction for the tabloids. When they performed at a political dinner in Washington DC, he met California congresswoman Mary Bono, whose husband, Sonny, had died in a skiing accident that same year. Brian chatted with her a bit about the slopes, and she gave him her assistant's phone number. The first time he used it, Mary took the call immediately. Their first date was picked up by the *Washington Post*, and in short order he was all over the news: *Access Hollywood*, *Entertainment Tonight*, and the *National Enquirer*, just for starters.

A few weeks later Diamond Rio was in Las Vegas to tape a television show when the publicist for the label stopped Brian from getting out of the car at the hotel. A mass of media had gathered to get photos—Brian was taken to a back entrance and snuck into his quarters.

"I was like a prisoner in my room the whole day," he says. "I'm talkin' to Mary on the phone, goin', 'Hey, what's goin' on here?' We'd had one, two dates, and everybody wants to talk to me. 'What do I say?' She said, 'Brian, just be yourself. Everything's gonna be fine. Don't worry about it.'"

"The only reason it became a big deal was because Mary was sitting on the Judiciary Committee that was in the process of impeaching Bill Clinton at the time," Brian continues. "So she was on TV every day, she's only been a widow for six months, and here she is dating the drummer with Diamond Rio, who has a reputation of being a ladies' man back in Nashville, and he's gonna break her heart—awful tabloid stories."

Brian, in fact, fell deeply—and quickly—in love and spent little time in Nashville for the next two and a half years. His typical week was to travel with Diamond Rio to concerts on the weekends, fly to Palm Springs to be with Mary on Sundays, join her on flights to DC on Mondays, then return

"This is Mary Bono and me at the top of the Rotunda of the Capitol Building in DC. What a spectacular view! Cherry blossom time in spring of 2000." —Brian

to Nashville on Thursday or Friday in time to ride the bus with the guys for another weekend. He took part in band meetings via phone, but even when Mary and he were apart, she seemed nearby.

"I'd be playing in the middle of Nowhere, Nebraska, and she's there with Colin Powell in DC, doin' an interview with Larry King, and I'm sittin' on the bus watchin' it before I go play a country music show in this dirt fair," he says. "It was surreal."

The travel didn't seem to bother Brian. But his wrists did. He developed carpal tunnel syndrome after all the years of slamming drum heads. He had surgery in California in November 1999, and his bandmates wondered if he might not stay in the Golden State when it was all over.

"I don't think any of us ever thought that Brian wasn't gonna be able to play," Dana says, "but it did run through our mind that Brian may just quit. He was so Mary Bono'd. Brian lives for see-and-be-seen, the social dude, to be out and amongst 'em and be at this event, get dressed for dinner and have wine with everything. Just that whole social scene— that's what Brian's all about, always has been. And brother, when he got with Mary Bono, 80 percent of her life is social, just one event to the other with famous people, or big political people, or whatever.

"I told Brian, 'Mary's absolutely perfect for you.' And I was glad for him, because that was the life he loves, and he was livin' it. And he was on a plane every week goin' back and forth to California to Washington, meetin' all kinda ex-presidents and actors and all kinds of stuff."

Brian took ten weeks to recover, but he didn't use the wrist injury as a point of departure. He rejoined the band in January 2000 for a show in Robinsville, Mississippi, as if nothing had happened.

"I missed him, man," says Dana. "I missed him as a player. I missed him bein' back there. He is, as much as anybody can be, rock solid, man, and you get used to somebody for all them years, you miss him. I did, and I'm sure it was a very scary time for him."

Brian and Mary got engaged, though the relationship faded in 2001.

By the end of that year, he was married to Stephanie Bentley, who wrote Faith Hill's "Breathe."

"That period I spent with Mary was the most fulfilling and rewarding time of my life," Brian says. "We don't talk often anymore, though I still count her as a friend. She opened me up to some new things—I thought about politics in a way I had never considered it before; I was meeting ex-presidents and movie stars, flying on Lear jets. Plus, she had two children with Sonny. They were great kids, and being around them brought an element of parenting to my life I had never experienced before."

"ONE MORE DAY" PHENOMENON

Just before that relationship ended, Diamond Rio experienced the biggest record of its career. They recorded "One More Day" in the spring of 1999, though it waited more than a year and half to be released. They intended it as a love song, and it certainly was that—though it proved to have even larger ramifications.

© Beth Gwinn

2001 With the songwriters of "One More Day" at the Palm in Nashville. *Left to right*: Brian, Steven Dale Jones, Dan, Bobby Tomberlin, Jimmy

"My first inkling of that was Shawn Paar, a radio guy in California, and a golfer—a guy I've played golf with," Marty recalls. "He told me when he got it at the station and played it, he at the time was divorced and had a son that was eight or nine years old, and he said he just took off for an early lunch and went to school and had lunch with his son. It just really hit him about cherishing the moment you have and making the most of it."

When ten people associated with the Oklahoma State basketball team died in a plane crash in January 2001, Oklahoma City radio station KXXY blended TV news bytes with "One More Day" to create a memorial that received play across the nation. When Dale Earnhardt died the following month, a similar tribute was paid to him, once again using "One More Day" as the centerpiece. Marty wasn't even aware of the Earnhardt version until it played on the radio as he drove a rental car to the funeral in Charlotte. Diamond Rio got press out of it, though they didn't generate any of it.

"In our industry, people see somethin' like that and the label people and the publicists, they wanna grab a hold of it and just carry that ball as far as they can," Marty says. "We were like, 'No, if people wanna do that with this song, that is great. I'm glad it meant something to them in some way, but we don't need to be profiteering off of that.'"

"Father/daughter dance at her [Mattie's] wedding. Full of emotion . . . dancing to the song I wrote for her." —Gene

The band did do a remixed pop version that brought more exposure on adult/contemporary radio stations.

As much as it meant to their listeners, the song was burdensome for a couple of the band members. When Diamond Rio met fans before their concerts, some fans had extremely emotional stories to relate about how "One More Day" had carried them through difficult family deaths or breakups. Jimmy felt overwhelmed at times by the stories.

Gene's daughter, Mattie, had a son, Benjamin, in July 2001, and doctors discovered during the delivery that she had cervical cancer. Of course, "One More Day" reminded him of his daughter.

"Every show, we're doin' it and making a special place in the show for it," Gene recalls. "I could barely get through."

Mattie's cancer was successfully removed.

© Beth Gwinn

2001. Gold Party at Label for "One More Day." *Left to right*: Butch Waugh (Sony Music), Ted Greene (Manager/ Dreamcatcher Artist Mgmt), Dan, Brian, Joe Galante (Sony Music), Gene, Marty, Dana, Jimmy, Mike Clute (co-producer), Bobby Craig (Arista Records/VP National Promotion)

"One More Day" found yet another new meaning when terrorists flew planes into the World Trade Center and the Pentagon on September 11, 2001. Within days radio stations across the country used the song as a reminder of the Americans lost in the attack. If anyone missed the connection, they were certain to pick up on it during the CMA Awards in November, when a video that featured images from the tragedy played behind Diamond Rio's performance of the song. Among the images, oddly enough, was a picture of Congress—including Mary Bono—on the steps of the Capitol.

The band couldn't see the backdrop at the time. In fact, Diamond Rio was doing everything it could just to get through the song—several guys were having trouble hearing. But they knew when the song finished that something magical had happened. An ovation began in the front of the Opry House, where the biggest stars were seated, and it spread like a wave across the floor and throughout the balcony. During the commercial break, the band was led back to its seats, past the star cluster in the front row.

"Shania Twain stood up—and tears are rolling down her face—and shook every one of our hands as we're walkin' by," Brian recalls. "Alan Jackson and Kix Brooks and Ronnie Dunn—and Barbara and Janine, their respective wives—they're in tears. And Denise Jackson, Alan's wife, is in tears. Everybody in the front row, all the big stars, they all stood up and just shook our hands. It wasn't so much 'Great song, great job, great performance'—just 'Thank you.'"

WRAPPING UP A DECADE

It was a stunning development. Diamond Rio had, that very same year, celebrated a decade since "Meet in the Middle" started their journey—at least in the public eye. The band's evolution had, of course, begun much earlier, in the early 1980s.

That they were still together after all this time was in itself an accomplishment. Plenty of softball teams can't keep egos aside long enough to make it through a season. In an industry prone to self-congratulation and inflated self-importance, each of the guys had maintained a high enough respect for the others to, at times, put his own interests aside for the greater good. Now they had earned their biggest hit after a decade in the Top 10—a length of time most acts never experience.

"Honestly, when we were starting our career, I had dreams that I was changing the world with my music, that somehow or another we'd have these songs that were powerful—if not life changers, little epiphanies in your life," Marty says.

"I dreamed about that, but by 2001, I have to admit I was somewhat cynical about the business. *That's not what it's all about and that's not gonna happen.* You just try to have some hits and make a bunch of money. Go figure. 'One More Day' sneaks up, we didn't plan any of that. I had a piece of material that has done it for a lot of folks, and that's been gratifying to me, to have something that's a little deeper and sticks with people. Fortunately we were able to have 'I Believe' a couple of years later, and it has done a lot of similar things for a lot of folks."

Marty would have a personal epiphany of his own just around the corner. It would take him several years to understand it, and it would put Diamond Rio's very existence on the line.

chapter 10

TEAM RIO

*N*ear the end of every year, Diamond Rio sends out Christmas cards to more than one thousand people, but it's not just a wish of glad tidings—it's

a card with a purpose. The picture on the front of the card is the handiwork of a child in the Big Brothers Big Sisters program. The band holds a contest among the kids every year—guided by a theme such as "What does Christmas mean to you?" or "What would peace

on earth look like?"—and the winner not only supplies the card design but also receives a gift card to fund holiday shopping for his or her family.

The back of the card features agency information about Big Brothers Big Sisters in both the U.S. and Canada, a way for Diamond Rio to increase awareness of its number-one charity.

GIVING BACK AND PAYING FORWARD

Lots of country artists talk about the value of giving back to the community: Diamond Rio is adamant about allowing others to piggyback on their own good fortune. They demonstrated just how important community involvement was to them when they first earned national recognition in 1991. Diamond Rio had started as the Tennessee River Boys eight years earlier. "Meet in the Middle" marked the beginning of monetary success for the group, though the initial returns were comparatively small. Dana Williams was, in fact, blown away to get checks for five hundred dollars two weeks in a row.

"That's two thousand dollars a month!" he laughs. "This was a job! I just couldn't imagine—I was blown away."

A five-hundred-dollar-a-week income is merely twenty-six thousand dollars annually, and yet even in those early days, Diamond Rio was already scheming about how to raise money for other people. Or to be specific, one other person: Glen Tadlock, their bus driver, was suffering from tuberculosis, and as the medical bills piled up, his dire reality hit home.

"We dearly loved this man," Dana says, "and so we thought, *Man, how can we help him?* So we come up with this idea: what about us havin' a golf tournament to benefit him and the bus drivers? And so with the first tournament, we were able to donate to him, like eleven or twelve thousand dollars."

On their way up, most of the guys had received some kind of aid from friends and relatives, and they already understood the value of a helping hand. Dan Truman had been given a place to stay for free by a series of friends—including Marty and Robin Roe—when Wendee had to move back to Utah while they dug out from under their own medical debt. Jimmy Olander's father subsidized his income when he was struggling just to pay the rent in the mid-'80s. Gene Johnson was given a place to stay by numerous fellow band members during his days in bluegrass, and Marty watched his father find jobs for many of his relatives when they were down and out in Ohio.

Brian Prout went through some very lean years when he worked the club circuit in Florida, and he still feels a certain indebtedness to a since-deceased acquaintance, who handed him six hundred dollars, no strings attached, when he needed it to pay his rent.

"When I had the money to pay him back, I contacted him," Brian says. "'I've got your money.' 'No, you don't.' 'Well, yeah, I owe you.' 'Brian, you don't owe me anything. You pay it forward. You will have the opportunity some day to help someone else out. That's what you do with it.' And ten times over, I've been blessed in return."

Golf Tournament

That first golf tournament, held at the Two Rivers Golf Course near Opryland, was only the beginning of a focused series of fund-raisers that have benefited both individuals and larger organizations. It became an annual event and, with Glen's TB as a starting point, it became associated with the American Lung Association. Plenty of stars came out to play—Kenny Rogers, Joe Diffie, Neal McCoy, Aaron Tippin, and NASCAR driver Tony Stewart, among them—and the tournament became a marker on the Nashville fall calendar.

"They've always had a lot of support from their celebrity friends," Modern Management's Renee Behrman-Greiman says, "and that's really made a lot of difference for us because it helps you bring in more players. They're excited about playing with celebrities, and it takes it to a new level."

The tournament was originally Marty's idea—understandably, because he's an obsessive golfer. He lives at the edge of a golf course in the Nashville area and *Golf Digest* ranked him in 2008 as the third-best player among musicians in the U.S. with a 0.2 handicap.

Brian is likewise an avid golfer, and Dan dabbles in it. The remaining members of the band have zero interest in the sport, yet they found ways to make the tournament an annual success. In addition to performing at the tourney concert, they drove drink carts around the greens and played host. Jimmy also skydived onto the course to kick off the day—once injuring his thumb during the landing badly enough that he needed surgery.

"Jimmy," Renee laughs, "has actually sacrificed his body for many a charity, let me tell you. He's lost toenails and torn ligaments too."

After the first year the tournament grew quickly, usually generating seventy to eighty thousand dollars annually. It also drew the attention of Arby's, which partnered with the band and brought in even more money. They soon were handing over checks every year in the neighborhood of one hundred seventy thousand dollars.

Bill Thorup

"Hey, I think I can see my house from here!" —Jimmy

Along the way Diamond Rio had brought in a second beneficiary, Big Brothers Big Sisters of Middle Tennessee, a mentoring program that matches needy kids with adult role models. Early in their career they had done a magazine piece at Six Flags Fiesta Texas that helped bring awareness to Big Brothers. As it turned out, one of Marty's friends, Bill Faith, had been a "Little" when he was younger, and Renee became a "Big" around the time she joined the Rio organization. The band saw firsthand the difference the agency could make in the next generation of the community.

"You got six guys and you got six different opinions about everything, but we all seem to have the same opinion about these causes that we wanted to help," Dana says. "When we found Big Brothers Big Sisters, it's like, hey, what better cause can you do than to help 'em from the beginning before they get screwed up?"

Initially Diamond Rio split the proceeds from its golf tournament between the American Lung Association and Big Brothers Big Sisters, although the second organization quickly became an easier fit with the guys, mostly because it reflected the importance they placed on family in their own lives. In a rather difficult decision, they ultimately ended their affiliation with the American Lung Association, in great part because concentrating their efforts on one agency seemed to have the largest impact.

"Our goal," Marty says, "is to try to find something that we are really connected to—not do a lot of different things, but just do one or two things that we are passionate about and we're really involved in."

Renee's attachment to her "Little," Sarah, had a major impact on the band. Sarah lived in a housing project just a block or two from abundant Music Row. Sarah's mom was raising her kids as a single parent. Renee would leave Post-it Notes on the door of their home to coordinate her visits with Sarah.

"You've never met a happier, more well-adjusted, positive child," Renee beams. "Literally the day I met her, she was this scrawny, cute, long-haired little six-year-old, and I walked through the door and literally fell in love with the child—big smile on her face, missing her two front teeth, the sweetest child you'll ever meet."

Sarah was about the same age as Marty's oldest daughter, Isabella, and Renee occasionally baby-sat Izzy and Marty's youngest—also named Sarah—or house-sat for Jimmy and Claudia.

"Never, ever once did my Sarah ever express jealousy or 'Oh, my gosh, they live in such big houses' or 'Oh, my gosh, look at all the toys!'" Renee says.

The Rio guys were impressed—and touched—by Sarah, and they reached out to her and her mom. They adopted her family for Christmas and also invited her to the group's annual holiday party for their own families, crew, and business partners.

The golf tournament continued to grow, and the Arby's corporate sponsorship became an unexpected blessing. The restaurant chain has a division that handles charity work full-time, and it freed Diamond Rio's management from spending massive hours doing things outside their expertise. The tournament also gave them an extra reason to form or grow corporate ties. When Hanes sponsored the Rio tour one year, the company made a major donation to the cause. Outback Steakhouse, meanwhile, doesn't sponsor tours, but they did cater dinners at the tournament.

Bill Thorup

Fall 2001. Annual Golf Classic to benefit Big Brothers Big Sisters. *Left to right:* (front) William Tichi (Executive Director, Big Brothers Big Sisters of Middle Tennessee), Sarah Fain (Renée's little sister), Annie McNeil, John (Sarah's brother) (back) Marty, Dana, Jimmy, Gene, Dan, Brian

In 2001 the tournament coincided with the terrorist attacks on September 11. The golfers started in the morning, around the same time the first plane hit the World Trade Center, which initially appeared to be an accident. The players headed to the course before the event was

Spring 2009. Sarah Fain graduating from Antioch High School. *Left to right:* Sarah Fain, Renée Behrman-Greiman.

fully understood as an attack and, with limited access to television or radio most of the day, they came to grips with the tragedy more slowly than people watching the news unfold at home or in the office. After some debate, Marty insisted the tournament continue. The terrorists were bent on crippling America; Diamond Rio and their friends were doing something to try and make a difference that day, and they would continue to honor that cause.

October 2005. The Arby's Charity Tour hosted by Diamond Rio was a two-day event that kicked off with a Sunday night concert, dinner, and auction held at the Wildhorse Saloon. A custom one-of-a-kind hand-painted Les Paul sold at the live auction for $3,700.00. *Left to right:* Greg Hawkins (ACT), Jimmy, Dana, Marty

Jimmy all along felt a little funky about the charities. They were a good idea—he wasn't disputing that—but he seemed to be getting great media coverage when he wasn't really that involved.

"I was the classic artist attached to a charity that had absolutely zero involvement with it," he confesses. "I can remember bein' at the Paso Robles Fair [in California] and Big Brothers Big Sisters showing up. I was told for a photo op, 'Get on this Ferris wheel with some Littles.' It just was so slimy that I was the national

2004. Marty playing his favorite sport.

spokesperson for Big Brothers Big Sisters and I basically knew nothing about it, but it probably made me look pretty cool.

209

"I rode that Ferris wheel, and I did these photo ops with these kids, and then they take the kids away. You pick up a magazine, you see me ridin' a Ferris wheel with some Littles, it's like, 'Well, geez, what a guy!'"

Jimmy was embarrassed about being a fake.

The Half Marathon and Team Rio

But Jimmy had the opportunity to correct that. Renee casually mentioned in late 2004 that she might run the half marathon—more than thirteen miles—during the Country Music Marathon in April. Deep down, she knew it wouldn't really happen. But Jimmy took her seriously and he promised that if she'd do it, then he would do it too. Suddenly she felt committed, then decided that if they were doing something that crazy, they might as well raise some money for charity. They got twenty-four people to enlist in Team Rio and raised more than twenty thousand dollars that first year for Big Brothers Big Sisters, with six to seven thousand dollars raised by one very aggressive runner.

Marty and Jimmy have regularly run the event with Renee since 2005,

© Pupak Photography 2009

5th annual Team Rio running and walking for BBBS of Middle TN.

and including 2009, it has brought in close to four hundred and fifty thousand dollars. Just as important, Jimmy has become a fighter for the Big Brothers Big Sisters cause.

"I'm so involved that I no longer have to, like the classic artist, get my deal-point memo where I'm cramming some fact to do an interview," he says. "I'm actually a supporter of the charity and know something about it, and it took me a long time to learn that there are so many more benefits to me personally and to how I feel emotionally about this whole thing, [knowing] that I'm doin' the right thing. I should've done this long ago."

Jimmy, despite his claims that he is not a runner, is a passionate recruiter. Beginning every fall, he tries to enlist people to run with Team Rio, looking for more money for the charity, convinced that the benefits he's received from being involved will rub off on anyone else who joins.

"You get so much more out of it than you put in," he says. "And you put in a lot. We'll run [almost] three hundred [practice] miles

© Elite Racing and Action Sports International

Jimmy O running 13.1 miles

by the time you get it done. Sounds incredible, but at the end of that deal it will have been empowering; you will have done something good for the charity and the journey. There's so many good people to run with."

Marty wavers a bit every year about committing, but invariably he takes part as well, creaky knee and all. His right knee usually begins making a cracking sound somewhere around mile six, likely from the friction of cartilage.

"It doesn't really hurt," he says, "but somethin' ain't right about that."

In the 2007 half marathon, Marty announced he was going to walk part of the way if necessary, so Jimmy held back on his pace to run

© Arby's Foundation, Inc., Courtesy of Arby's Charity Tour

Check presentation for the Arby's Charity Tour. *Left to right:* Brian, Dan, Ted Greene (Modern Mgmt), Gene, Lowell Perry (BBBS), Dana, Jimmy, Marty, Greg Hawkins (ACT)

alongside his friend. During the last half mile, Jimmy pulled ahead just a bit, but Marty noticed a female runner was lagging.

"She's totally dehydrated," Marty says, "and as I come past her, she starts to fall, and I catch her. Jimmy's a little ahead of me. He goes, 'C'mon, let's go!' Then he sees that I'm walkin' with this girl. It was about fifteen minutes 'til the First Aid got to her, 'cause she was not gonna make it. She couldn't hardly speak or anything."

"Anyway," he adds with a wink, "she killed my time!"

Once they crossed the finish line, Jimmy made sure he had a photo with Marty.

"Jimmy was afraid I wasn't gonna ever do it again," Marty notes. "And I haven't decided yet!"

Some of the other guys were insistent that they would not do the half marathon. Dana laughed off the idea, although his wife ran it in 2007. Dan has trained on a smaller level with his daughter, McKenzie, and has taken her to the kids' version of the marathon. Brian made it clear he was not participating.

Photos by Jaimie Ellis, Courtesy of Modern Management

Photos by Jaimie Ellis, Courtesy of Modern Management

2006. Country Music Marathon and 1/2 Marathon, Nashville, Tennessee. *Top*—Having too much fun? *Left to right*: Marty and Jimmy. *Bottom*: "Marty making it look so easy . . . I hate him just a little for that." —Jimmy

"Brian's like, 'I am not a runner, I am not a walker, I'm a biker,'" Renee laughs. "When Team Rio came up, he just basically called and said, 'You ain't wranglin' me into this. It ain't gonna happen.'"

© 2009 Grand Ole Opry Archives. Photo by Chris Hollo

Receiving the Minnie Pearl Humanitarian Award. *Left to right:* Porter Wagoner, Brian, Gene, Marty, Dana

© 2009 Grand Ole Opry Archives. Photo by Chris Hollo

October 15, 2004. Surprised by the Minnie Pearl Humanitarian Award presented on stage at the Grand Ole Opry House. *Left to right:* Pete Fisher (GM Grand Ole Opry), Brian, Gene, Marty, Steve Wariner, Dana, Porter Wagoner, Dan, Jimmy

March 3, 2005. "Surprise! You are the recipients of the Country Radio Broadcasters Humanitarian Award." The band thought they were on-site to present an award to Bobby Kraig with Arista Records.

March 3, 2005. Recieving the Country Radio Broadcasters Humanitarian Award at the Nashville Convention Center. *Left to right:* Brian, Dana, Brad Paisley, Marty, RJ Curtis, Dan, Jimmy, Gene

"As adamant as Brian was that it was too early, too many miles, the first year we did it he made a homemade sign and is standing on the side of Belmont Boulevard with his sign cheering us on. It was so sweet. Then he moved to the bridge, right before the bridge. People are crazy, traffic's crazy, and he is out there as excited as we are to be doing it. It's very sweet," Renee says.

For their efforts the band was surprised with the Minnie Pearl Humanitarian Award during an appearance on the Grand Ole Opry in October 2004. The following March they received a similar honor from Country Radio Broadcasters.

Not Always Public

Despite the acknowledgment, there's plenty more the public doesn't see, or that the guys simply choose not to promote. After doing mission work in his early years, Dan continued to build fund-raisers into his off hours. He's performed at benefits for the families of soldiers in the Middle East, as well as for women's charities. And he's worked with the Nashville Songwriters Association International, which actively fights to preserve the ability of composers to make a living from the songs they've created.

During the years that Arby's sponsored the Diamond Rio golf tournament, Dan also took part in an Arby's program that taught values in the school system.

"Dan is so amazing with children," Renee says. "He's a troop leader for the Boy Scouts. He gets involved in everything his children do, and he's so hands-on with the church and church programs. He doesn't always talk about it, but he's always doing something charitable."

Gene and June have likewise hosted numerous parties for Big Brothers Big Sisters, and they're active on a personal level with the Parkinson's Foundation. He prefers not to talk much about it.

"You should be doing things, yes," he explains. "It shouldn't always be public knowledge that you're doing them. And so sometimes I shy away

2004, Dan teaching values lesson at Ross Elementary School.

Left to right: Delmont Truman (Dan's dad), Dan, Ben, Chad, Casey

from that public side of it in favor of doing other things that are helpful and beneficial to those that need it and [choose to] not let people know about it."

Race Car Rio?

Not that Gene won't take part in public events. For several years, Diamond Rio members drove cars at the Tennessee State Fairgrounds in Mark Collie's celebrity race to benefit diabetes. During one of the races, Gene got caught in a jam going around the third turn on the track. Gene was riding alongside Ronnie Dunn, of Brooks & Dunn, who had quite a bit of experience racing. The car in front of Ronnie spun out of control, but Gene hung in, believing Ronnie would stick to the inside of the track.

"Just as I thought that, he pulled to the right and stuck his front wheel in front of my rear wheel," Gene recalls. "I was accelerating and it vaulted my car skyward."

Marty Roe literally drove underneath Gene while he flipped in the air. Gene's car quickly came down at the outside of the track, bashing into the wall and the pavement at the same time.

"It was," he says matter-of-factly, "a real abrupt stop."

Gene refused to go to the hospital, but when pain subsisted several days later, he visited a doctor, who diagnosed a broken tailbone and mis aligned vertebrae. He had to sit on a cushion with the center removed for weeks—making for some miserable traveling on the tour bus and plenty of jokes from the other guys.

Jimmy, organizer that he is, has begun the legwork to add another annual event to Diamond Rio's Big Brothers Big Sisters schedule, now that the golf tournament has run its course. And at least one of the guys may become more personally involved with the kids too. Tour schedules typically keep the band out of town on weekends, which are the most advantageous times to foster a Big-Little relationship with the Big Brothers Big Sisters program. Diamond Rio has purposely pared back its tour schedule to eighty to one hundred dates per year, and it leaves Marty able to make more time for mentorship.

"It's probably in [my] future," he predicts. "I never had a son, so that would fit me pretty good."

Ultimately the Team Rio concept fits Diamond Rio as a whole. Their success was built on hard work and perseverance, but they also recognize it was not accomplished on their own.

"The biggest part of getting a blessing is not keeping it," Brian says. "It's passing it along and paying forward, so to speak. That's meant basically just taking advantage of the blessings that we've had and the notoriety and the attention that the Diamond Rio name will bring to an event or a fund-raiser. It just seemed like the best way for us to reach out into the community and say we're not in this just for us."

© Arby's Foundation, Inc., Courtesy of Arby's Charity Tour

October 20, 2003. Presenting a check to Big Brothers Big Sisters of Middle Tennessee. *Left to right*: Gene, Jimmy, Bill Tichi (Executive Director, BBBS of Middle TN), Dana, Marty, Dan, Brian, Michael Lippert (COO, Arby's Foundation, Inc.)

© Arby's Foundation, Inc., Courtesy Arby's Charity Tour

2003 Arby's Charity Tour hosted by Diamond Rio to benefit Big Brothers Big Sisters of Middle Tennessee, Special Event at the Wildhorse Saloon, special guest NASCAR's Tony Stewart. "Tony was gracious enough to participate in the live auction (coming straight from a race earlier in the day) and brought one of his race suits, helmet, and jacket [to auction off] and he alone raised over $22,000.00 for the event. Tony's got a big heart!" —Brian

© Arby's Foundation, Inc., Courtesy of Arby's Charity Tour

October 2005. A special moment: Gene's 4-yr-old grandson Benjamin signed his auction paddle in the hopes of raising additional money for kids. The paddle went for a whopping $600.

© Arby's Foundation, Inc., Courtesy of Arby's Charity Tour

October 2006. Benjamin again wanted to do something for the little boys and girls, just like "PaPa" was doing. His CD brought $3000.

© Arby's Foundation, Inc., Courtesy of Arby's Charity Tour

2004. Brian working away! Anything for the kids. Members of Diamond Rio sold $1 pin-ups to benefit Big Brothers Big Sisters of Middle Tennessee.

L to r: Lowell Perry (CEO, BBBS), Marty, Jimmy. $120,000 for kids!

© Arby's Foundation, Inc./Courtesy of Arby's Charity Tour

L to r: Jimmy, Don Kendall (Board President, BBBS), Marty, Lowell Perry (CEO, BBBS), Gene, Greg Hawkins (ACT), Dan. $100,000 for kids!

chapter 11

NOWHERE BOUND

Photo by Señor McGuire

*I*n the wake of "One More Day" in 2001, Diamond Rio entered a new phase, one that outwardly signaled a revival. The band had been charting singles consistently for ten years and had now created its biggest hit yet in a career arc that had already lasted longer than most artists experience.

Combining talent, strong material, hard work, an all-for-one group mentality, and a little bit of luck, the guys had lasted longer than anyone could have—or should have—predicted. They were on an upswing. They had done it with a song that meant huge things to many of their fans. Internally, however, things were crumbling. The guys were still friends. They still respected each other. They still believed in each other's talents. But their concerts had started to slide.

SLIDING . . .

Marty began having pitch problems, and they soon escalated from the occasional bad show to mostly bad shows. For a band that was recognized as "meticulous"—as Storme Warren would later put it—the fall was demoralizing. There was no single defining moment when they slid from grace, no single night that Marty lost his mojo. It came on gradually, sometime on the road during 2001, when a song or two in the course of a concert fell out of pitch.

It had happened in the band's early days—at their first official Diamond Rio show in Ohio in '91 and again in Montgomery, Alabama, with Pam Tillis—before the guys had invested sixty-six thousand dollars in ear molds, the in-ear devices that had made it easier to hear. With that system they had reduced the clash of instruments that accompanied floor monitors that once were the standard for concert staging. But there still were moments when low sounds—particularly the drums—created some hearing problems. Under those conditions, it was not uncommon for a vocalist to push the volume to rise above the cacophony. The louder a singer got, the more likely he was to lose control of the pitch. So when

Marty began wavering on notes or hitting the occasional clunker, no one was too bothered.

"He always had this amazing pipe, you know, this great voice with its incredible range and that great throat, and every so often, he'd sing off pitch," Dan says. "It was usually when we were in a really uncontrolled situation as far as sound, and that's typical for a lot of people. You go to live concerts, and you hear—I've heard Billy Joel sing off pitch. I've heard all sorts of people sing off pitch."

"Most of the show was all right," Gene adds. "He had some problems with this song or that song. It was kinda disappointing, and when you'd get done, it was, 'Well, that wasn't a great show.' But you kinda just live with it, hope the next one's better. But it became more of a thing where every night *that* song was bad. It wasn't just once in a while that song was bad. Every night—he has a problem singin' *that* song."

"Gene and I, bein' we're the [harmony] singers, we felt the problem comin' probably a lot sooner than the other guys, I would think, just because we're singin' with him," Dana says. "So we started out real subtly: 'Hey man, you have trouble hearin' tonight?' It just kind of continued on and started gettin' worse. Then right out of the blue, Marty'd have a good night, and we never could figure out: 'Hey man, how can you have a good night here and be so bad all those other nights?'"

No one confronted Marty directly. Part of the reason Marty was such a successful lead singer for the group was his swagger. He oozed with self-confidence that he'd earned with his distinct sound and his willingness to take on the face-of-Diamond-Rio role that had been assigned to him. They knew that calling attention to his shortcomings was bound to bruise his ego, and they remembered well the Tennessee River Boys period in which Marty had been the least confident of the band's singers.

Rather than hitting him squarely with the problem, they continued to drop hints and hope he'd figure it out on his own. He didn't—or at least he didn't let on that he knew. And the band was at a loss as to how to fix it.

"No one in the past had ever been in denial about anything—especially like that," Dan says. "We would always talk through a matter, take care of it, make a decision, and put it behind us. And this thing, we couldn't get him even to see what was goin' on."

Complicating it all was the uncertainty of music itself. If they had been accountants, it would have been cut and dried; they either balanced the books or they didn't. If they were construction workers, it would have been easy to assess—the ditch was dug, or it wasn't. Here it was much more hazy. Music is ephemeral, a group is a big collaborative effort, and the other collaborators—particularly the harmony singers, Gene and Dana—began to doubt both themselves and Marty.

"I heard the trio in my head and it was off," Gene says. "Even though I was pretty sure it was Marty, it also made me question myself, and as time went on I had to question myself for good reason. If you're tryin' to sing with somebody and they're singin' off-key, you're probably not gonna be on.

"Having been a harmony singer—specifically a tenor singer—all my life, I'm used to tuning things. When you hear something isn't right, you move [the pitch] slightly to try to make it right, so I guess that was one of the painful things that we went through. I was tryin' to correct the things that I couldn't correct. It made me doubt myself."

Marty showed no signs of self-doubt, and as the band became bolder in addressing the issue, it created friction. The other members became more discouraged and withdrawn, particularly after a bad show. After the encore, they'd take out their ear molds, put their instruments in their cases, and head back to the dressing room—or the bus—to change.

Avoiding a Tough Issue

"You're startin' to take your boots off, startin' to change back into shorts and a T-shirt, and there's this silence," Jimmy says. "Do we need to talk about this? Should I say, 'Hey, you did that one song okay'? Is that going to be interpreted that all these other songs were horrible? Do you just let this alone?"

Invariably, someone found another subject—a weirdly dressed fan or the backstage food—and the group avoided the real issue.

"I didn't wanna talk to Marty after a show," Gene says. "I'd kind of get changed and get off in my own space."

Recording Challenges vs. Live Performances

Russ Harrington

Released 2002

Once the note was delivered on stage, it was gone for good. In the recording studio, the problem could be fixed before the public heard it, and in the early stages of Marty's vocal issues, Diamond Rio recorded the *Completely* album, notching two more number one hits, "Beautiful Mess" and "I Believe."

On previous projects Mike Clute typically recorded three or four vocal performances of a song from Marty, then compiled the best segments of those recordings into the final product. It was a standard operating procedure in Nashville studios, and Marty was actually easier to record than many of his peers in other acts.

But on *Completely*, the process was much more laborious. Clute amassed forty to fifty versions of Marty singing each song, then "comped"— as they say in the business—the best pieces together. Clute also brought in several vocal coaches—including Robin Wiley, who'd worked with Justin Timberlake and Britney Spears—to aid Marty in the studio.

The recordings were, admittedly, better and easier than the concerts, in part because they had multiple opportunities to get it right before anyone heard the results. "It was kind of like gettin' on a different bike, hearin' tracks [through studio headphones] versus live," Clute says. "I think he was always able to step up to the plate a little bit better in the studio, even though we had to work harder. Those are some really passionate tracks and great performances, and he did 'em."

Painful Playbacks

Nothing seemed to help Marty with his denial about the live shows. To nudge him toward the truth, the band finally came up with a unique intervention. They started recording every live show and listening to it on the bus. Rather than singling Marty out, they made it a group effort. All of them would gather in the lounge and play back the entire set, grueling number after grueling number.

"You do this seventy-five-minute show that you've been doing all year long, what's the last thing you wanna do?" Jimmy asks. "Sit down and listen to the seventy-five-minute show. And a really bad one too."

The process was painful and embarrassing. It wasn't long before Marty stopped listening with the rest of the guys. He continued to play the CDs on his own with headphones, avoiding his bandmates' faces.

"It was tough on him," Dan observes. "It was way tough. I'm right across from him in the bunk [on the bus], and he would take those CDs to bed with him, he'd get in his bunk, and he'd listen. All of a sudden, you could tell. All of a sudden, he was gettin' it. But it was I don't know how many months into it—ten, twelve, fourteen months into it—he was finally getting it."

"I don't know how many tears he'd shed back there by himself," Dana says. "I'd left all mine on the stage. I was all dried up."

Even at that, Marty remained resistant.

"I didn't feel like it was as serious a problem as what everybody else was portraying it," Marty says. "And some nights were better than others. It improved slightly, I think."

227

Self-Coaching

Long before Diamond Rio signed its first contract, Marty had given voice lessons to his fellow singers at Opryland.

"When you try to stylize something in country music, you don't really sing [technically] right," Marty says. "The stylization of doin' an Ernest Tubb [impression] or somethin' like that, it's very pinched, and if you do that five times a day and you do several artists like that, it's hard on your voice."

Marty reasoned that with his knowledge of the process, he could work out the problems on his own. He'd stopped warming up years ago and decided that was the biggest issue.

"I would sit in a bathroom behind a hall someplace," he recalls, "and warm up for an hour or more, just vocalize—probably overdid it, I'm sure—and then I went to points where my voice would get tired."

With his voice now ragged and fatigued, his spirit drained from sixty minutes of focused singing, Marty would deliver another seventy-five-minute show with only slight improvement. He began to pressure himself. He hung on every good show as if it were a turning point and wallowed in the bad ones. He began to have as many doubts about himself as the rest of the band.

"I've always been pretty relaxed on stage, and during this time, I was not," Marty says. "I felt like I was kind of under a microscope."

The tension mounted for everyone on stage as his partners overcompensated in their attempts to show support.

"Every little twitch" was a potential setback, Dana says. "We could just be singing, and if I just winced because a bug hit my eye—or whatever—he'd come over to me and, 'Am I singing bad?' 'No, man, just a bug flew in my eye.' I mean, we went through a long period where he just couldn't be comfortable. Now the paranoia has set in."

It was evident when Marty would turn from the audience to get a swig of water from the bottle at the edge of the drum stand. He had a problem, he didn't know what to do about it, and his pride was sinking in front of his friends and in front of thousands of people every night.

"I could just see the anguish in his face," Brian says. "And from my angle, 'cause we keep the drums off to the side of the stage kinda between where Marty is and where Dana stands, Marty would turn his head while he's singin' or tryin' to hit some of these notes. I could tell; it was like he was in pain while he's tryin' to hit these notes. And of course, I'm back there thinking, *Please don't try to hit that note again.* Marty, just bein' the kill-the-beast, drag-it-home kinda guy—'I can do it. I can go for it.' 'No, you can't.'"

The more Marty tried, the more he pressured himself, the worse things became.

"Goin' to do shows was an absolute dread," Marty says.

Turn It Off!

He eventually agreed that he couldn't solve the problem on his own, and he started seeing vocal coaches. They made some impact, but not enough to rescue Diamond Rio's live performances. The rest of the band, their attitudes spiraling downward, started having the engineer take Marty's vocals out of the mix in their ear molds. It didn't improve the product they were delivering to audiences, but they had to do something for self-preservation.

"It was very common to see Dana or myself motioning over to the monitor board," Gene says. "All we had to do was make a cut sign where you slash your hand across your neck, and they knew what we wanted."

"When I gave that signal, that meant, 'Turn it off.' Not down. *Off,*" Dana emphasizes. "I'd always start every night very optimistically. Then pretty much every night, I'd make it about four to five songs—if I made it that far—and I couldn't hang no more. I looked at the soundman, and he pretty much knew what was comin'. I just couldn't."

After a time, neither could the soundman. Johnny Garcia ran the board at the band's concerts, and he had to listen to each of Marty's performances all the way through. It was discouraging because the bulk of the shows had become so ugly. Johnny dropped Marty's vocals down to a minimum level, so that many nights the other instruments drowned out his voice in the venue's speakers. Johnny was doing his best to salvage Marty's reputation, though he was harangued at many of the concerts by the people in the seats.

"He's out there sittin' in the audience where people can interact with him," Jimmy says. "People can harp at him and stuff—'But I can't hear the lead vocal!' He can't say it, but he's thinkin' in his mind, *Yeah, it's a good thing.* It was particularly tough on him."

Johnny eventually left Diamond Rio, discouraged by the parade of deflating shows.

"People take pride in their jobs, and he hung in there very, very, very long, until he just couldn't take it anymore," Jimmy says. "And I was like, 'Man, I would've quit long ago.'"

Disappointed Fans and Friends

Johnny might have taken the brunt of it, but the band members heard from the fans too—sometimes indirectly. During one performance in front of forty thousand people in Grand Junction, Colorado, Marty had a particularly bad show. By the time they got back to the hotel, Brian was frustrated and decided to get away for a beer. He went to a nearby restaurant and sat at a bar, where three fans still wearing their wristbands from the concert sidled up next to him. They didn't recognize Brian and they didn't hold back.

"They just got into this thing," Brian recalls, "of 'Boy, Diamond Rio sucked! They sounded awful. That singer can't sing. It must be all that studio stuff that they do.' Then the other guy said, 'Well, I saw 'em two or three years ago and they sounded great. I don't know what the problem was today, but that was awful.'"

Hearing the fans complain was painful, but it was even more heart-breaking when their fellow artists started dropping comments. Vince Gill, for example, had sung with Marty on demo sessions in Nashville during the Tennessee River Boys era. He knew what Marty could do with a song.

"We did a show with Vince one time," Dana says, "and we were sittin' at catering, and he just offered up a voice teacher. Just right out of the blue: 'Hey, man, I heard this voice coach . . .' right out of nowhere. Then we did another show with Marty Raybon [of Shenandoah]. We got done with the show, and Marty come up to me and just wanted to talk—'So what's goin' on with Marty's voice? I can help him.' This stuff come totally unsolicited, you know. I'm like, 'Well, I really wish you could help. 'Cause it's killin' me.'"

Nothing Physical

Marty went to the Vanderbilt Vocal Center to see if there was something physically wrong. The facility, headed by Dr. Robert Ossoff, is one of the leading throat clinics in the nation and has been helpful to many country stars, including Kathy Mattea, Ricky Van Shelton, Sara Evans, Patty Loveless, John Michael Montgomery, and Josh Turner. Vanderbilt has solutions for all kinds of throat-related issues—from deviated septums to vocal lesions to allergies—including preventive techniques and, in the worst cases, surgery.

As it turned out, Marty had some hearing loss, but nothing out of the ordinary for a working musician. There were no physical problems, which meant his tortured performances had become a psychological issue. It also meant they couldn't leave the road. Had Marty needed time off for vocal rest, they could have easily canceled some dates, given him the time to recover, and then gone back out. But without a medical issue, they couldn't legitimately back out of their tour commitments.

Complicating matters, they were a group—not a solo act. The artist's share of concert profits for any given date went into six bank accounts, instead of one. There were six band families—as well as the families of other managers and employees—all relying on Diamond Rio to finance more health concerns, more college educations, more automobiles than the typical country artist. They couldn't really afford to stop working.

Reworking the Set List

Instead, Diamond Rio attacked the set list. A number of songs— "You're Gone," for example, which had become unbearable—were bounced from the show in favor of less-demanding titles. Some of their signature songs couldn't be pulled, so instead, they dropped the keys and reworked the vocal assignments. "Meet in the Middle," which they'd traditionally played in E, was now shifted to the key of D; and on the choruses, Dana started singing Marty's parts, with Marty in turn taking the lowest part of the harmony.

"It was a smack in the face," Marty confesses. "But it definitely made our show quality better, which was the most important thing to all of us—for buyers to feel like they were gettin' their money's worth and our audiences to feel like it."

They also began for the first time employing a vocal tuner, a computer that helps adjust pitch automatically. They used not one, but two tuners, and even that step failed to completely correct the problem.

"He could sing so far off that the tuner would move it to the wrong note," Gene says. "Say he was supposed to sing an A—it went to B because he was closer to the B. That does not help out front. You couldn't make the tuner correct for as off as he was."

As bad as things had gotten, it seemed it was only a matter of time before the band imploded. This was, as Storme Warren had noted in their 2005 GAC special, a "meticulous" group. They had set high standards for themselves, and they were consistently failing to deliver.

Marty "wouldn't have made it through *American Idol* and gone to

Hollywood," Jimmy says. "This vocal wouldn't have made the choir in high school. You're not even singin' in the same key. This isn't just a sour note; it's as bad as it could be."

Life After Diamond Rio?

Morale was low, the guys dreaded hitting the road, and they no longer felt like a group. Most of them began to contemplate life after Diamond Rio. Jimmy figured he would become a session guitarist, Dan started talking about teaching piano lessons again, and Gene mulled the possibility of returning to the less-lucrative bluegrass field. In fact, Gene mentioned the idea of quitting at the band's management office, he'd become so depressed about the direction Diamond Rio had taken. Jimmy talked him out of it—rather quickly, in fact—but the band's demise began to have an air of inevitability.

"It's not like I was in a big rush to leave," Gene says. "I wasn't jumpin' up the first time Marty sang off pitch. It was suffering through years of it and not seeing the light at the end of the tunnel. For me, it was 'I don't want to ride it back down.' I have more pride than that."

No Band Change—All or Nothing

While the rest of the band wasn't leaving, they never pushed Marty to leave either.

"We never went there," Dan says. "I think we knew that to find somebody like him was gonna be tough. Also when you get a new singer, it just changes the whole dynamic of everything. We never addressed that. We just knew we either needed to help him get it back, or we were gonna have to change our life. We wouldn't change the band."

By 2005, Diamond Rio was doing repeat business with promoters who'd paid for poor shows the previous years, and the truth was becoming more clear to the outside world. When the vocal problems first hit, they could gloss over it a bit, and they certainly did.

Russ Harrington

"I don't like to admit to lying, but we definitely sugarcoated the story," Marty says. "I didn't, 'cause someone else was coverin' for me in the office, or in the band—'Oh, he's just gettin' over a cold' or whatever. I don't know what they told 'em, but it wasn't the true story."

Promoters might have bought it the first time, but when the band used the same story a year or two later, the concert buyers began to suspect something was up.

"Our crew guys would come to us and tell us, 'The promoter, man, he thought we sounded awful,'" Dana recalls. "A couple of 'em would come and say, 'Hey, what's wrong with Marty, man? This is the second time I had you guys. He sung terrible the last two times.'

"You'd get some people who'd go, 'Sounds like Marty's lost it, man!' And other industry people that we've known through the years, they knew who and what it was. That was the real issue, man. We'd go play these big festivals, have all these other acts on there, and we'd get up there and just stink."

Arista Says Good-bye

By the time 2006 rolled around, Marty was past the denial stage. He knew there was a problem. He no longer felt it could be fixed. Adding to the tension, Arista had declined an album they submitted in 2005. In its place, they released a second *Greatest Hits* project with "One More Day," "I Believe," "Beautiful Mess," and a few new songs— plus, rather oddly, their first single, "Meet in the Middle."

The album was all but ignored at retail, and Arista dropped Diamond Rio from the roster, sadly ending a fifteen-year relationship.

"We weren't surprised," Dana says. "They kinda spelled that out for us, slowly but surely. They sure went the long way around the block, but they did spell it out for us."

Released 2006

CARING ENOUGH TO CONFRONT

Gene had a friend who had helped him as a vocalist. Marty had even met her a few years earlier at a wedding. Gene was convinced she could aid Marty. Thus far, Marty had been resistant, but with the band's opportunities sinking, Gene caught Jimmy's ear.

Jimmy O was, in essence, the group's organizer, and he also roomed with Marty on the road. He knew Marty better than anyone and was the band member most likely to get a positive response from their singer. So Jimmy called Marty in hopes of taking one last swing at a vocal coach. The conversation started poorly. Marty conceded that he was having trouble, but he insisted that all the focus on his voice by his bandmates was only increasing the pressure. He was practically afraid to go out on stage.

"Well, what am I supposed to do?" Jimmy asked. "I'm tryin' to help you. I can't pretend the problem's not there. It's in my best interest—*your* best interest—that we fix it, but you're tellin' me if I talk to you, it's makin' it worse? What do I do? If I don't talk to you about it, we continue and just ignore it, it doesn't get any better."

It was at that moment that Marty broke down in tears. He'd made a very good living with his voice, but it no longer worked for him, and he doubted he would ever be able to sing properly again. Marty recounted to Jimmy a well-known parable found in the Gospel of Matthew. In the story a wealthy man takes a trip and leaves his finances in the control of three servants. Two of the servants invest his money—or "talents," as the translation says—and increase his bank account. The third buries the talents in the ground. When the wealthy man returns, he takes the talents from the third servant and gives them to one of the other two servants, who earn his praise.

"When the master came back, he was pleased with the first two and displeased with the last one," Marty told Jimmy. "I feel like I've done that with my gift. I don't know if I've got more than one gift, but I know I've got that one. And the master's taken that one talent away."

As a youngster, Marty had once been so fearful of singing in public that he couldn't finish a song when the audience clapped in the middle of the performance. The pendulum swung the other way during his ascent as a professional—he'd grown so completely confident that he would sing entire shows out of tune and believe he'd done well. Now his spirit was broken. He'd worked with a number of vocal coaches, none of whom had an answer. No one was really certain if Marty's problem could be fixed.

But Jimmy had a suggestion: "I've got somebody else for you to see."

chapter 12

REVIVED

Russ Harrington

*A*nswers come in the oddest places.

The solution to Marty Roe's vocal problems—and, thus, the solution
to Diamond Rio's issues—was already in place. It just took some time to
figure it out.

In 1999, when Gene Johnson's daughter, Mattie, got married, it drew a new personality into the band's orbit. Diane Sheets was best friends with the groom, Dave Gallagher, who was working as a background vocalist in Nashville's Christian music industry. Diane and Dave had sung together as teenagers in a group that traveled to churches in Columbus, Ohio, and the surrounding area—much as Marty had done during his own teen years in Dayton.

WEDDING SINGER

Diane sang at Mattie's wedding, where she first met Marty and the other Diamond Rio members. She also met Jimmy Olander during a rehearsal for the ceremony at his house. Claudia was playing piano at the time, and Jimmy—after greeting Diane—viewed the practice session as dimly as he had viewed the Tennessee River Boys years earlier, when he took the job only because he needed it.

"I just kinda blew her off," Jimmy confesses. "'This is beneath me, I'll be down in the studio. Excuse me, people, rehearsing for a wedding?'"

Gene and June, however, had a different response from their experiences with Diane at the wedding. They called her after she returned to Columbus and told Diane that if she wanted to explore moving to Nashville, they'd be happy to let her stay in their home.

In short order she was able to transfer with the insurance company where she worked—with a four-thousand-dollar annual raise. She stayed with the Johnsons long enough to get situated. A year after her arrival in Music City, she got a job with a music publishing company that worked directly with Word Entertainment. Diane was unable to stay, however. Her grandparents were ailing, and she returned to Columbus to see them through their final years. Back in Ohio, she was introduced to Estill Voice Training, a program that blended physiological science with the art of singing.

Estill Voice Training

She went through an intense training program, and Gene became a guinea pig of sorts. He was surprised at the results: even after thirty-plus years of singing professionally, he was helped by Diane's Estill-bred coaching methods.

"It's all based on your muscles and how you use them to effect what you want," Gene says. "It's really steps away from the old vocal coaching techniques. It actually contradicts a lot of what they used to do."

As he learned more about the process, Gene was convinced Diane could help Marty. He consulted with Dana and Jimmy, and Jimmy was elected to float the idea to their lead singer, who was so broken he was willing to try anything.

Diane came to Nashville August 15, 2006, with a pair of physicians from the Ohio State University Medical Center and conducted some preliminary tests on Marty, Gene, and Dana to get a full picture of their vocal cords, throats, and nasal passages, and she stuck around to see a private performance they gave for a corporate conference at Opryland.

Marty talked with her a bit before that show, though he was "sort of grumpy," Diane says. And he pointed out that he already knew he had some hearing loss—not unusual among musicians who spend their lives performing in front of large speakers on a regular basis. The show itself was an unmitigated disaster. After just three songs—"Beautiful Mess," "Bubba Hyde," and "Unbelievable"—it had already turned into a painful experience.

"It was horrific," Diane recalls. "Marty was terrible. And when they did 'One More Day,' I realized that none of them were listening to each other. They weren't hitting the same spots that they needed to, there was no blending happening. It was like three singers singing on stage to their own music. Nobody was listening to each other."

That was literally true. The other guys had, after all, resorted to turning

Marty off in their own ear molds. As a result the audience shut off the entire band.

"At the beginning," Diane says, "they [the audience] were really happy to see Diamond Rio. By the end nobody was listening, everybody was milling about. It was embarrassing."

Once the test results were back, Diane returned to Nashville on October 4 to meet with the band once more. The first morning she had an appointment with them at the office of Joe Bennie, their accountant, to discuss their physical issues—which were practically inconsequential—and to develop a program to get them back on track. While Marty was en route to the meeting, Robin called manager Ted Greene in a panic. Marty, she said, was extremely depressed and felt as if the band was ganging up on him. They needed to work through the process with kid gloves, Ted relayed to Diane. Then he left her in the conference room to sort out the mess.

Diane and the three singers went through some preliminaries, and then agreed that Diane would work with Marty on day one, with Gene and Dana set to return the next day. Once the other two were gone, Marty froze on her. She suggested lunch. He scowled, folded his arms, and eventually prodded her to step it up.

"Why don't we go ahead and get started so we can get this thing over with," he told her.

She suggested they do a few warm-ups with some instrumental tracks Mike Clute had put together for her. Marty rolled his eyes.

"You've already heard me sing," he said. "What do you think my issue is?"

Diane took a deep breath and then eased into it.

"Well," she hesitated, "this may sound strange to you, but it's your tongue."

"What?" Marty was incredulous.

"The tongue," Diane explained, "is attached to the larynx, and the larynx is where your vocal cords are, and you tend to fatten the tongue up in the back of your mouth a lot. You sing high notes, and your larynx has to rise to sing the higher notes. You're trying to control the tone, but you're really fighting against yourself. You're making it harder. You just kinda need to relax and stop trying to control it so much, just be free with the tone."

Marty had done voice coaching before, and he'd seen several coaches in the last few years. No one had offered such a weird solution, and he certainly wasn't buying it now.

"That's ridiculous," he scoffed. "I don't do any of that."

He tried to bring the whole thing to a close. He'd already consulted a gaggle of established voice experts in Nashville. He needed to fix his vocal cords, and she was talking about his tongue. He wanted an answer, but he didn't believe this was it.

"It's over," he said.

So much for the kid gloves. Diane, shocked at her own assertiveness, leaned over the table and shot right back: "Why don't you lose that attitude for five minutes, Marty. You've been nasty to me since I walked in this door. I'm here to help you."

Twenty-Minute Challenge

"What do you have to lose?" she continued. "Give me twenty minutes of hard work, and if you don't feel a difference after that twenty minutes, we'll call it a day and all that you've lost is twenty minutes of your time. I won't even charge you. I'll let management know it's not gonna work, and I'll walk away. You don't lose anything."

Marty stared at her for a bit, then got up and left the room. Diane was shaking. She didn't talk to people that way and was uncomfortable with the feeling. She sensed it was, as he had said, over; she packed her things to leave. But before she got to the door, Marty returned with two glasses of water.

"I was despondent," Marty says. "I was broken. If I didn't have my best social skills on, I can see where it would be perceived as antagonistic.

It was not toward her; it was toward the fact that I had to be there, *period.* That I had gotten myself to that point."

Marty gave Diane the twenty minutes she asked for, and he focused hard. He gave her his complete attention, did everything she asked. The twenty minutes turned into an hour. Then two hours, three hours passed.

"'Just talk these songs'—that was her metaphor or analogy," he remembers.

Diane was able to demonstrate to him that, in fact, he was letting his tongue get in the way. It was a symptom of the pressure he'd put on himself. He was trying so hard to correct himself that he made the situation even more intense.

"I was tight in the throat and very tight in the diaphragm," he says. "When it was time to sing the high note in 'Mirror Mirror' or 'Meet in the Middle,' everything would tense up and revert back to a wrong spot."

By the end of the session, the tension between Marty and Diane had completely dissolved. In fact, he asked if he could take the practice tapes home so he could demonstrate to Robin how much progress he'd made.

Gene and Dana showed up the next day, with Jimmy along to play chords. The three singers ran through their material. Unlike the corporate show at Opryland, they were all in sync, with the same instant blend they'd experienced back in 1989 when Dana auditioned in Brian's garage.

Marty's Back!

"It was like night and day," Dana says. "It was just unbelievable, the change that happened in him."

Jimmy pulled out his cell phone in the middle of rehearsal and called Claudia at home: "You're never gonna believe it. We've got the old Marty back."

On day three, the entire band met at a rehearsal hall with Diane and their soundman, and they launched into their typical set list. Once again, Marty was out of tune, and he instantly reverted to the old cynicism.

"It was terrible," Diane recalls. "He kept saying, 'See, I told you this wasn't gonna work.'"

Diane talked Marty into letting her hear the in-ear mix he had worked out with the technician. She was stunned at how little of the Diamond Rio sound was available to him.

"The only thing he had in his monitor mix was his voice, high hat, and his guitar; and it sounded like a tin box," she says.

Marty had been so concerned about his hearing loss that he overcompensated in the high frequencies in his headset. A handful of popping, sibilant consonants—"f," "p," and "t"—overpowered everything else.

"You can't find pitch center like that," Diane says.

She had his personal mix reset to standard levels, and they tried again. This time Diamond Rio sounded just like—Diamond Rio. The band was overjoyed. They went through the set list *twice* that day and felt they had conquered a demon.

"Diane just worked wonders," Brian says. "I think as much as physically teaching Marty how to sing again and do it properly, I think she helped him with his psyche, with his mental state."

"He's back now," Dan agrees. "He's got this incredible voice—it's a little older, but boy, he's got all that power back. He's at 98 percent of

Left to right: Marty, Brian, Jimmy, Diane Sheets, Gene, Dana, Dan.
"Diane . . . our career saver." —Jimmy

what he was, and some nights he's at 100 percent. That's awesome because he used to be at 30 or 40 percent."

LOOKING BACK

In hindsight, Marty was able to retrace his fall. Early in the band's career, he'd been pushed to take on the voice-of-Diamond-Rio role. The interviews were a bundle of extra work, the band had allowed itself to do a ton of dates, and he'd simply burnt out on major parts of the job. He'd grown so cocky that he stopped warming up before concerts; and when on the road, he would literally play golf all day, show up at the backstage area with little time to spare, shake a few hands, then walk out and sing.

Since he wasn't singing unless he had to, he periodically lost control of his voice. He tried to fix it by pushing harder, which only made things worse. When he got the hearing diagnosis, he treated it like an elixir and overreacted. As Diane had discovered, it only made the problem worse.

"Most people study their instruments," producer Mike Clute explains. "They spend a lot of time practicing, even when they've mastered it, to keep growing. If you only play for the shows or whatever, you're probably gonna start to get pretty stagnant. The thing with [Marty's] voice, he only had to sing when he had to sing. He did it reasonably well enough to keep [up for a time], but he wasn't really stretchin' it, wasn't looking after it or analyzing it."

"Face it," Clute adds, "if they would've had the typical country career, they would've been done in five years and none of this stuff ever would've mattered. You never would've noticed it."

By the time Marty got his vocal problem fixed, Diamond Rio had plenty more than five years of public history under its belt. The group had survived *fifteen years* on the frontline and still wanted more.

LOOKING FORWARD

With their old singer back, but no recording contract, they decided they had a free hand to try whatever they wanted. First, they went in the studio and recorded a bunch of songs they'd considered over the years but had never actually done. Next, they tackled a Christmas album—something they'd always talked about but never gotten around to. Diamond Rio recorded *The Star Still Shines: A Diamond Rio Christmas* with the old swagger and tight harmonies. Because it was a seasonal project, it allowed them to step outside of the stylistic boundaries that typically guide a mainstream country album. The CD included some bluegrass, some jazz, some smoky torch textures. And it got the attention of Word Entertainment, which signed on to distribute the album, then extended the deal to include a Christian project.

"One More Day," "I Believe," and "In God We Still Trust"—a song the band had included on its second *Greatest Hits* album—all demonstrated their spiritual values. Word figured it was not a stretch to bring them on board. Plus, the label had a relationship with Warner Bros., so it was possible to take an appropriate Word release and work it as a

Russ Harrington

Released 2007

single to country radio. They signed the deal in the spring of 2008, though after the ink dried, both sides realized it was an unusual match.

"At all the Arista parties, used to be they'd break out the tequila," Gene laughs. "Especially in the early Arista days it was a small company, big partiers. When we signed with Word Records, I don't think there was any tequila."

The label, meanwhile, pointed out during a brutally frank meeting with Jimmy that the Christian market would view them skeptically. They needed to be able to explain why they had shifted from country to Christian music. As the conversation ran its course, Jimmy felt for the first time that there had been a divine hand guiding them through Marty's vocal problems and to Word Records. Diamond Rio had a story to tell about real conflict and redemption. Marty would be key to making it work. It was essential that he be willing to share his journey.

When Jimmy got home, he retreated to his studio downstairs. He remembered growing up in California and Michigan, how his father, Bill—a confirmed agnostic—had forbidden Margie, Jimmy's mother, to take the boys to church. Bill was angered at his own religious upbringing and held a firm skepticism about spiritual issues. In spite of his father's rules, Jimmy had somehow been a believer; as a child, he prayed in the darkness of his room and never told a soul. As he considered how far off course the band—and he—had gone, Jimmy prayed there in his studio for forgiveness and reconnected to the Spirit he had overlooked for years.

He consulted with Clute and the band's managers, then gave Marty a call.

God at Work

Jimmy didn't expect the conversation with Marty to be an easy one. Marty had denied his vocal problems for years; now Jimmy would be asking him to come clean to the entire world—a humiliating task, to say the least. Jimmy pointed out the irony that the one guy in the band who had exhibited the least spiritual tendencies was the one who had received an epiphany. He believed they had gone through their turmoil and gone to Word for a reason.

Marty agreed that there was a bigger force at work. He remembered the confrontation with Diane in 2006. The band's meticulous reputation had been compromised by his own inattention to his talent and by his stubborn belief that he could fix himself. He opened the door just enough to let God—working through Diane—set him back on course.

"I believe," Marty told Jimmy, "God has put us on a path that has brought us to this place where we're gonna do something that's bigger than us."

With that opening, Jimmy suggested that Marty's shortcomings, and his subsequent renewal, could be the key to that path. But, Jimmy noted, Marty would have to put himself in an uncomfortable situation to pull the whole thing off.

"He was not thrilled by what I was asking him," Jimmy recalls. "I could tell by the silence on the phone."

After a long pause, Marty finally responded, "What do you want me to do?"

Jimmy challenged Marty to write about his experiences, put together some songs that illustrated the grace he'd found and share it with their audience. By the time the conversation was done, they had agreed that for the first time, Diamond Rio would make an album that told its personal story. The two of them proceeded to write the first song for the project, "The Reason," which became the title track.

Something to Say

Four of the guys—Marty, Jimmy, Dana, and Dan—each contributed at least one song, many of them addressing the issues they'd faced as a band. They had "refound" their gift, renewed their spirit, and discovered they had something to say.

"For the first time in memory, success is not what's turnin' our crank," Marty says. "We're a little more puristic about our music and our reason for doing it. No matter what comes along, Diamond Rio is gonna be a band playing music that we love."

247

The guys challenged themselves as songwriters, and they challenged themselves as musicians. They experimented with two-part harmonies at times, instead of their typical trio; put harmonies in places they might not have used them before; added instrumentation and electronic effects that were atypical; and even considered an outside musician or two to influence the tracks, something they had never done before.

They ultimately used only extra musicians who played instruments the band did not. They had always intended to record songs in a way that they could reproduce them on stage, and they decided to maintain that principle.

But entertaining the idea displayed an appropriate flexibility on the part of the band. Marty had been willing to allow an outside source, Diane Sheets, to infuse a little new energy, and she helped him regain his old form. Maybe the whole band could benefit from musicians and ideas that came from outside their usual sphere of influence.

"We could all stand a little more reenergizing," Gene says.

As a result, the album is a bit of a departure. Jimmy O's guitar sound has more of a classic-rock texture, the lyrics are more emotional than visual, and some of the melodies take on the soaring arc of typical pop songs. All the while, Gene's harmonies and shreds of mandolin still hold Diamond Rio's feet firmly to the band's country roots. It's a place from which big things can happen. And indeed big things have happened in the individual lives of the band's members since 2002, when the vocal crisis first hit Diamond Rio.

PERSONAL CHANGES

Dana

Dana came to the realization that he and Lisa had been growing apart for years. With a steady stream of money coming in from his work on the road, Lisa quit her job in 1992 but hadn't really found a new motivation in life other than the birth of Jacob in '96. When Dana came in from Diamond Rio tours, he frequently retreated to his computer and they stayed in opposite parts of the house.

"I probably wasn't the best husband in the world," he admits. "I know I wasn't. I was gone all the time, and I got to feeling that I had two lives. I had my road life and I had my home life, and I don't know, we were just gone so much. We literally just coexisted instead of [being] husband and wife."

Their minister counseled Dana that if he hung in, the passion would eventually return. But he suddenly felt a spark for a longtime friend, Deanna, that had not been there before. During the ACM Awards one year, Dana ran into Billy Dean. They talked for more than two hours, and Billy relayed a bit of wisdom that another man had given him: "You never know how big a hole you have in your life 'til somebody starts to fill it."

"Deanna and I just arriving at our new home after our wedding. I was just about to carry her across the threshold. Man, those were a lot of stairs!" —Dana

Deanna was filling places in Dana's heart he had not realized were vacant. She was what he had been looking for, and Dana told Lisa he felt

"Our family Christmas picture 2008. Chris, Deanna, Cara, me, and Jacob. Miracles do happen!" —Dana

it was time to end their marriage. She offered little resistance and, in fact, is on good terms with Dana and Deanna.

"I ask the Lord every day for forgiveness for it," Dana says. "I feel better and I'm happier; *we* are happier, life is fulfilling, the whole thing. I mean, I wanna do everything with Deanna. Everything feels right. And if I did wrong, as far as in God's eye, then that's why we have forgiveness."

"I don't know," he says with a shrug. "That's heavy stuff for me, 'cause I don't get heavy very often."

Some of Diamond Rio's songs—including "One More Day"—now have much greater meaning for Dana.

"Every night I talk to Deanna on the phone when I'm gone," he says, "and I talk to her a half-dozen times a day probably. And every night she says, 'Sing me a song.'"

Dana's response is invariably the same: "I'll always sing 'One More Day' to you."

Dana remains close with his parents, Maurice and Louise, and sister Scarlet, who still live nearby. "I thank God every day for their continuous influence on my life," he says.

His marriage to Deanna expanded Dana's family. In addition to his son, Jacob, he now has a stepdaughter, Cara, and stepson, Chris. Like many of the families that are part of Diamond Rio's fan base, he is both a supporter and chauffeur for his three kids and their band concerts, football games, and basketball games.

Dana and Deanna opened a retail store, the Trendy Trunk, in Hendersonville, Tennessee, with Scarlet and her husband, Tony, in April 2007. Dana can be spotted there periodically changing lightbulbs or hauling out the trash.

In addition, he's started an advertising business with a friend.

The computer, which was once an escape for Dana, has now become a significant hobby. And the boating accident that nearly took his life has not dimmed his affection for the water. The family still enjoys trips to the lake during the summer.

"You should see Jacob ski," Dana boasts. "He makes me so proud in so many ways."

Dana has dedicated himself to keeping a close-knit family, and they make an effort to have their dinners together, with each member of the clan sharing something about the day at work, school, or play.

"In the end," he says, "these are the most important things in life. God is blessing this family every day."

Brian

Brian went through a divorce from Stephanie Bentley, whom he married in December 2001. The couple had a daughter, Lily, on September 25, 2002, and had twins—Bentley and Sophie—born four months early in January 2005. Brian had previously resisted fatherhood and was stunned to find at age forty-six how much it meant to him.

"It was the most amazing moment of my life," he says. "I'd have done it twenty years ago if I had known."

Brian and Stephanie parted ways in 2007. The loss of another relationship hurt, but the separation from his children was particularly painful.

"Jimmy," he recalls, "said something after this episode with Stephanie: 'Brian, did you ever consider the fact that maybe it's you?' I said, 'Believe you me, buddy, I have.' I really think that there's something inside of me that I can't finish the deal. I can get so far in a relationship and support it and be a part of it and find a lifeline in it for myself, I just don't know that I can go the distance."

"That was tough to accept for a while," he adds, "but I took some time to readjust my dreams, and at this point in my life, I'm fine to be alone."

Not that he's a hermit. Brian is inherently social, and he connects often with friends in Nashville when Diamond Rio is not on tour. He also makes at least one annual pilgrimage to Utah to ski during the winter months. The weather and the mountains are an extreme version of his boyhood home in upstate New York. The skiing is cathartic, and he hopes eventually to retire in Utah.

"I always feel like I'm able to play in God's backyard and He's okay

Brian at the base of Mt. Timpanogas, Sundance, Utah—Sundance Ski Resort.

with it," Brian explains. "It's the scenery and the cool air and the snow—it's beautiful. I've never really been able to describe to anybody the depth of feeling when I get off the chair lift and stand there at the top of the mountain before I take the run down. I take deep breaths and marvel at the scenery and how it changes with the sunlight during the day. There's just nothing nicer than a very heavy snow day, where it's snowin' so hard you can barely

Nashville, Green Hills Mall. Brian, daughters Lily (6) and Sophie (4), Santa, and son Bentley (4).

see 100 yards down the road. It's fun. It brings out an element of bein' a kid and wantin' to get out there and play in it all day."

That memory of his own childhood innocence has also been a huge aid as Brian adjusts to the realignment in his adult family. No matter what discomfort he experiences in being separated from his children, the kids and their future are still the most important thing in his life.

Gene

More than thirty-five years after Gene and June married, the family has expanded. They have a pair of grandchildren, Benjamin and Nicholas, who've been an inspiration on a pair of fronts. Gene has begun mentoring the boys to play mandolin, and June has begun writing a series of children's books that are currently placed with an agent.

2009. "Me and June . . . still in love."
—Gene

"She's always been a great story-teller," Gene says, "and my daughters and I finally convinced her to put them on paper. What started out as a naptime story for our grandsons has turned into a really wonderful book."

The series now numbers three titles, with the first called *Wellman's Lot,* which has much significance in Gene's family. It's the name of a fifty-two-acre plot from his family's original land back in New York. Gene's brother, Dick, passed away several years ago; and his sister, Hazel, recently sold her share of the farm and moved to Pennsylvania. As a result, for the first time in more than one hundred years, no one from the Johnson clan is living on the Sugar Grove plot.

Nevertheless, Gene still has a connection to his homeland that serves as a daily reminder of his roots. He harvested lumber from Wellman's

2009. "My family. *Front:* Mattie Sam, Benjamin, Nicholas, me. *Top:* June and Callie Jo." —Gene

Lot to build new wood floors in the living room and hallway of his Nashville-area home. In addition, he hand-built wooden cribs for Benjamin and Nicholas that will one day be family heirlooms.

"It's where I'm from and part of who I am," he says. "Who knows? Maybe the boys will be the next generation to build from Wellman's Lot."

Gene also used wood from his land to construct a home studio, where he recorded all his mandolin and harmony parts for the new album and Dana added some of his

"At home in my wood shop."
—Gene

harmonies. Gene also intends to use the studio for his own bluegrass projects. In 2009, he started work on one of them—a reunion album by Night Sun, the band he worked with in the mid-1970s when he moved to Nashville the first time.

The entire family—kids and grandkids included—eats together almost every week, with June frequently putting together a big spread. They've also begun visiting a local Mexican restaurant, and their relationship with the waitstaff exemplifies Gene's ability to conduct his life without showbiz pretense.

"There's usually at least ten of us that walk through the door," he says. "They have no idea who Diamond Rio is, but they love my family, and more than half the staff calls my wife 'Mama!'"

Jimmy

Jimmy has undergone massive personal changes. He and Claudia, after years of insisting they wanted no children, did a complete reversal. They adopted two kids, Max and Tank, and have found a new life richer than they could have ever imagined.

Franklin, Tennessee. "My family with Judge Easter at our adoption finalization for Tank. This is moments after we pulled up in front of the courthouse and proceeded to lock Tank and the car keys in the SUV. Luckily, since we adopted both boys, none of our less-than-brilliant biological genes have been passed on." —Jimmy

"I've had a life full of jumpin' out of every kind of airplane you can imagine," he says. "I've jumped off of a cliff in Brazil hang gliding, [become a] member of the Grand Ole Opry, won award shows, gotten to know some of my heroes on a first-name basis. I've had some really exotic things happen to me in my life.

"After all that, where do I want to be? What is the most rewarding part of my life? Claudia and the boys. That's the real stuff. Now in the mornings, I walk Max to the end of the driveway where the school bus picks him up, and we throw a football around. Or we'll make breakfast waffles for dinner and watch *Frosty the Snowman* in July when it's boys' night and Claudia needs a break. Or Tank, my youngest, will tell me what his latest superhero power is and then proceed to try to disappear—or, as he says, 'dis-rah-pier.' It's just incredible."

Jimmy also came to feel a need to be closer to his parents. He encouraged them to move to Middle Tennessee, and they now live just a couple of miles away, allowing the boys to have a strong relationship with "Gah Gah and Papa."

Jimmy is best recognized as the band's guitarist, but he's branched out in other ways professionally. He's become more prolific as a songwriter, picking up such non–Diamond Rio cuts as "The Night Before (Life Goes On)," which appeared on Carrie Underwood's *Some Hearts* album; and Kenny Chesney's 2000 hit "I Lost It." He's also built a well-kept studio in his home and begun producing a couple of new acts.

Miranda Taylor

Left to right: Max, Claudia, Jimmy, Tank.

"In spite of all the great things and unexpected joy that have come my way, my best work, most fulfilling loves, and the greatest years of my life sit in front of me," Jimmy maintains. "I can just feel it in my bones."

Dan

Even away from the band, Dan is constantly engaged with music. Two of his kids, Ben and Chad, have formed a duo—Truman—that's received some overtures from pop labels. Their typical set list includes a popped-up version of "Beautiful Mess," and they signed with a Nashville booking agency for tours. They are, in effect, at the same point in their career that Dan was when the Tennessee River Boys were pushing ahead diligently in the late 1980s. Dan's formed a music publishing company, Truman Show Music, to manage the copyrights for the duo and for his own side pursuits.

Dan and a longtime friend, Nashville guitarist Ron Saltmarsh, have recorded a couple of smooth-jazz albums, providing a creative outlet for some expertly crafted music that doesn't really fit Diamond Rio's style or game plan.

Dan's daughter, McKenzie, was a nice addition to the Truman household after three boys. She has a beautiful smile and has developed a quick,

Photo by Matt Clayton

Truman

cutting sense of humor. She has a natural gift for speaking in front of an audience and, like the other members of the family, sings and plays music with loads of enthusiasm. Son Casey, who put up a video called "She Made Me Waffles" on YouTube, was set to start church-related mission work in the summer of 2009.

The biggest change in Dan's life was the most difficult, and it took great amount of introspection before he consented to reveal it in a book. Facing unforeseen challenges, Dan and Wendee ultimately ended their marriage, and the divorce was being finalized in 2009.

2008. "Benjamin graduated from BYU's Marriot Business School with honors, then took his business degree and immediately started playing music full time." —Dan *Left to right:* Casey, McKenzie, Ben, Wendee, Chad, Dan

"Four incredible kids hangin' out at the Pancake Pantry in Nashville." —Dan *Left to right:* Chad, Casey, McKenzie, Ben

Dan remains thankful for Wendee's extraordinary skills as a mother and longtime support as a friend. He is optimistic that the two of them will each make a successful transition over the long term and that his children will benefit from their parents' willingness to deal honestly with their relationship.

Marty

Marty and Robin teach a group of teens in a church-related covenant group, just one of numerous activities in the Roe household. They've been counselors for the same group of kids for five years and have a hand in their progression from junior high through high school.

Marty might be the famous member of the household, but Robin has shown a wide range of talents as well, both at home and in the community. She did a massive amount of intricate work in decorating the walls of their suburban home. She also directs the teen praise band at church and has teamed with Lana Thrasher—whose husband, Neil, has cowritten a number of Diamond Rio songs—to create an album of Christian songs. Robin and Lana use the album to support their work at women's conferences in churches across the United States.

Their daughters, Isabella and Sarah, are both in their teens and beginning to form their own lives apart from Mom and Dad. Izzy begins college in the fall of 2009, while Sarah starts high school.

Marty's dad underwent open-heart surgery in December 2008. His recovery went extremely well, and Marty still takes his family to see his parents in Ohio as often as possible.

"They have always been a steady place to land when life is getting rough," Marty says. "We love getting to visit them at every chance. I can't begin say how wonderful it has been to share our success with them. God has been good to them, and I have definitely been a benefactor of that."

Marty and a neighbor, JT Olson, have founded an organization

Sarah Roe   Isabella Roe

called Both Hands, built around the concept of providing one hand to
widows and the other to orphans. The agency, which tells its story at
www.bothhandsfoundation.org, has developed a unique sponsorship

Todd Media/Springboro, Ohio

2006 Roe family photograph. *Left to right:* nephews Dylan and Clayton,
brother Scott, sister-in-law Anne, parents Bertie and Zane, Robin, Marty,
Isabella and Sarah

2009—the Roe family

structure to fund the cost of upgrading widows' homes while defraying the expenses of qualified families looking to adopt children.

Marty and Robin are putting their faith to work in the community and enjoying a personal relationship that has now lasted more than twenty-five years.

"That," he says of their longevity, "is my greatest blessing."

TWENTY YEARS AND COUNTING

January 2009 marked twenty years since Dana became the most recent new member of Diamond Rio. That track record—two decades without a single lineup change—is practically unheard of among groups, and it's a testament to the mutual respect the guys have for one another as musicians and as people.

The music business is littered with stories of bands that broke up over jealousies, money issues, creative disagreements, short tempers, or—in the most common instance—one member deciding he is bigger and more important than the group.

That hasn't happened with Diamond Rio for multiple reasons. They decided, back when they were still the Tennessee River Boys, to give everyone an equal financial share in the partnership. They also initiated the no-women-on-the-bus rule, carving out an inner sanctum where they know they can work through issues without the additional voices of their wives.

But each of the guys also brings important personal characteristics to Diamond Rio that have made it function so smoothly. Growing up on the farm, Gene learned teamwork early by doing whatever it takes to make things work out for the family. Jimmy originally moved to Nashville with a plan to become a session player, but he gave that up when he discovered the camaraderie that accompanied the Tennessee River Boys. Dan's work in college and at Opryland taught him the value of blending his musicianship into a larger whole. Brian had, from his early days as a musician, always wanted to be a member of a successful band. Dana simply could not resist the tug of playing in a group. Marty's initial lack of confidence had made the River Boys the perfect starting point for his career, and by the time he got an offer to go solo, he was completely committed to his partners.

"We've all struggled together," Marty says, "and because of that, it's easier for us to stick together, I think, in the good times. I have great respect for everybody's contribution and everybody's sacrifice."

Diamond Rio is comprised of six very different guys. They've endured their share of tugging and pulling, but they're each willing to put their individual needs aside to guarantee the group's survival. There've been no public spats, no defections, no irreconcilable controversies, because their commitment to each other supersedes their desire for personal attention.

In concert, every member of the band gets at least one moment to stand out, but in the end, Diamond Rio is about blending. It's apparent in every song they've cut in their two decades as a recording act and particularly evident in their biggest hit, "One More Day." Marty might be the lead singer, but the harmonies are so seamless they sound as if they come from one mind. There are instrumental moments between the vocals in which the guitar, piano, and mandolin interweave so subtly in supporting roles that they work almost as a single instrument. The bass and drums are simple—no grandstanding, just the right accents to underscore a message of commitment.

Commitment is, in fact, a recurring theme that's been present often in their music, from "Meet in the Middle" to "Walkin' Away" to "Imagine That" to "I Believe." And commitment is something they've lived out professionally in a way that few bands have managed.

It's been a long road. The guys' early years were a struggle; they hit some glorious heights, and—had they been just about any other six-person group—they likely would have imploded when Marty went through his toughest professional moments.

But Diamond Rio isn't just any group. They had the tenacity and the will to stick it out, and they share a depth of dedication that transcends anything they could have imagined.

Diamond Rio's story is a beautiful mess. And an inspiration for anyone who wants to know what's possible when a small group of people rolls up its sleeves and works together.

appendix A

DIAMOND RIO'S
TOP 20 COUNTRY HITS

Billboard Peak	Radio & Records Peak	Title	Month of Chart Debut
1	1	Meet in the Middle	March 1991
3	3	Mirror Mirror	July 1991
9	5	Mama Don't Forget to Pray for Me	November 1991
2	1	Norma Jean Riley	March 1992
7	4	Nowhere Bound	July 1992
2	2	In a Week or Two	November 1992
5	4	Oh Me, Oh My, Sweet Baby	April 1993
13	9	This Romeo Ain't Got Julie Yet	July 1993
21	15	Sawmill Road	November 1993
2	1	Love a Little Stronger	May 1994
9	8	Night Is Fallin' in My Heart	October 1994
16	15	Bubba Hyde	February 1995
19	15	Finish What We Started	May 1995
2	1	Walkin' Away	December 1995
4	3	That's What I Get for Lovin' You	May 1996
15	17	It's All In Your Head	August 1996
4	2	Holdin'	December 1996

1	2	How Your Love Makes Me Feel	June 1997
4	4	Imagine That	November 1997
4	4	You're Gone	May 1998
2	2	Unbelievable	October 1998
1	1	One More Day	November 2000
18	15	Sweet Summer	May 2001
1	1	Beautiful Mess	April 2002
1	1	I Believe	November 2002
16	15	Wrinkles	August 2003

(Sources: *Billboard* chart positions compiled in *Joel Whitburn's Top Country Songs 1944 to 2005*, *Radio & Records* magazine)

Russ Harrington

How Your Love Makes Me Feel Video Shoot

© Deaton Flanigen Productions

© Deaton Flanigen Productions

Stuff Video Shoot

© Deaton Flanigen Productions / Photos by Steve Lamar

© Deaton Flanigen Productions / Photos by Steve Lamar

© Deaton Flanigen Productions / Photos by Steve Lamar

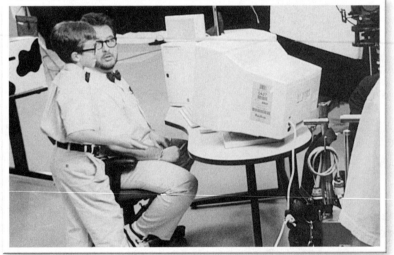

© Deaton Flanigen Productions / Photos by Steve Lamar

One More Day Video Shoot

© Deaton Flanigen Productions / Photos by Steve Lamar

© Deaton Flanigen Productions / Photos by Steve Lamar

© Deaton Flanigen Productions / Photos by Steve Lamar

© Deaton Flanigen Productions / Photos by Steve Lamar

Beautiful Mess Video Shoot

© Beth Gwinn Courtesy of Deaton Flanigen Productions, Inc.

© Beth Gwinn Courtesy of Deaton Flanigen Productions, Inc.

It's All In Your Head Video Shoot

Courtesy of Deaton Flanigen Productions

1996, Martin Sheen on set.

Courtesy of Deaton Flanigen Productions

Left to right: Brian, Gene, Ramon Estevez, Jimmy, Martin Sheen, Marty, Dan. "I met Ramon down on Music Row while doing some demos, and he soon became a good friend of my entire family. Through that friendship we were able to have both he and his dad appear in our 'It's All In Your Head' video. It was a thrill to watch them work together." —Gene

I Believe Video Shoot

© Deaton Flanigen Productions / Photos by Steve Lamar

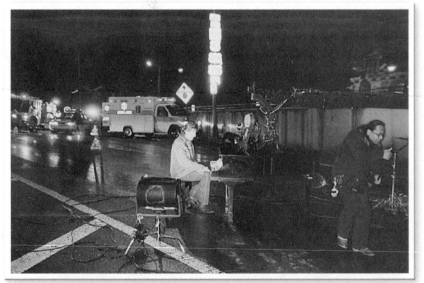

© Deaton Flanigen Productions / Photos by Steve Lamar

© Deaton Flanigen Productions / Photos by Steve Lamar

© Deaton Flanigen Productions / Photos by Steve Lamar

In God We Still Trust
Video Shoot

Renée Behrman-Greiman Courtesy of Modern Mgmt

Renée Behrman-Greiman Courtesy of Modern Mgmt

Renée Behrman-Greiman Courtesy of Modern Mgmt

Renée Behrman-Greiman Courtesy of Modern Mgmt

Renée Behrman-Greiman Courtesy of Modern Mgmt

appendix B

DIAMOND RIO'S MAJOR
AWARDS AND NOMINATIONS

Year	Award (Show)
1991	Vocal Group of the Year (CMA)
1991	Best Country Performance by a Duo or Group, "Meet in the Middle" (Grammy)
1991	Best Country Instrumental Performance, "Poultry Promenade" (Grammy)
1991	Top New Vocal Duet or Group (ACM)
*1991	Top Vocal Group (ACM)
*1992	Vocal Group of the Year (CMA)
*1992	Top Vocal Group (ACM)
*1993	Vocal Group of the Year (CMA)
1993	Best Country Performance by a Duo or Group, "In a Week or Two" (Grammy)
1993	Album of the Year, *Common Thread: The Songs of the Eagles*, Various Artists (ACM)
1993	Top Vocal Group (ACM)
*1994	Vocal Group of the Year (CMA)
*1994	Album of the Year, *Common Thread: The Songs of the Eagles*, Various Artists (CMA)

* Award

Year	Award (Show)
1994	Best Country Instrumental Performance, "Appalachian Dream" (Grammy)
1994	Top Vocal Group (ACM)
1995	Vocal Group of the Year (CMA)
1995	Vocal Event of the Year, "Workin' Man Blues" with Lee Roy Parnell, Steve Wariner (CMA)
1995	Top Vocal Group (ACM)
1996	Vocal Group of the Year (CMA)
1996	Best Country Performance by a Duo or Group, "That's What I Get for Lovin' You" (Grammy)
1996	Best Country Instrumental Performance, "Big" (Grammy)
*1997	Vocal Group of the Year (CMA)
1997	Best Country Performance by a Duo or Group, "How Your Love Makes Me Feel" (Grammy)
1997	Single Record of the Year, "How Your Love Makes Me Feel" (ACM)
1997	Video of the Year, "How Your Love Makes Me Feel" (ACM)
1997	Top Vocal Duo/Group (ACM)
1998	Vocal Group of the Year (CMA)
1999	Vocal Group of the Year (CMA)
1999	Best Country Performance by a Duo or Group with Vocal, "Unbelievable" (Grammy)
2000	Vocal Group of the Year (CMA)
2000	Top Vocal Group (ACM)
2001	Single of the Year, "One More Day" (CMA)
2001	Vocal Group of the Year (CMA)
2001	Best Country Performance by a Duo or Group with Vocal, "One More Day" (Grammy)
2001	Best Country Album, *One More Day* (Grammy)
2001	Single Record of the Year, "One More Day" (ACM)
2001	Song of the Year, "One More Day" (ACM)
2001	Top Vocal Group (ACM)

* Award

Year	Award (Show)
2002	Vocal Group of the Year (CMA)
2002	Best Country Performance by a Duo or Group with Vocal, "Beautiful Mess" (Grammy)
2002	Top Vocal Group (ACM)
2003	Vocal Group of the Year (CMA)
2003	Best Country Performance by a Duo or Group with Vocal, "I Believe" (Grammy)
2003	Top Vocal Group (ACM)
2004	Vocal Group of the Year (CMA)
2004	Home Depot Humanitarian Award (ACM)
2004	Top Vocal Group (ACM)
2005	Vocal Group of the Year (CMA)
2006	Top Vocal Group (ACM)

(The "year" represents the primary eligibility period for the award. The Grammys and ACMs are presented the year after eligibility. For example, the ACM trophy for Top Vocal Group was presented in 1992 for the band's work in 1991.)

© cj SHELKER

Diamond Rio accepting the award for "Vocal Group of the Year" at the 1997 CMA Awards (Nashville, Tennessee).

© cj SHELKER

ASCAP Awards 1994. "One of my oldest and dearest friends, Eric Silver accepting his first ASCAP award for a song we wrote, 'This Romeo Ain't Got Julie Yet.' " —Jimmy
Left to right: Merlin Littlefield (ASCAP), Marty, Eric Silver, Jimmy, Dana, Brian, Connie Bradley, Gene, Dan

2004 CMA Awards, Nashville, Tennessee. It was a family affair on the Red Carpet.
Left to right: Gene and daughter Mattie, Dana and son Jacob, Marty and daughter Isabella, Dan and son Chad

On the Red Carpet in Las Vegas, Nevada, for the 2005 Academy of Country Music Awards.

2005 Academy of Country Music Awards in Las Vegas, Nevada. Presenting the "New Artist" award with Jamie O'Neal.

© Tim Parks NASCAR Scene

September 4, 2003. Diamond Rio celebrates Tony's win in Victory Lane after the Truck Race at the Richmond International Raceway.

© Tim Parks NASCAR Scene

September 4, 2003. Marty, Dana and Jimmy hang out with Tony pre-race at the Craftsman Truck Series Race at the Richmond International Raceway.

© Tim Parks NASCAR Scene

Left to right: Jeff Weimer (band friend), Dana, Brian, Gene, Jimmy, Marty. Diamond Rio cheering on Tony at the Craftsman Series Truck Race, Lowe's Motor Speedway.

© Tim Parks NASCAR Scene

May 20, 2005. Diamond Rio minus Dan sings the National Anthem at the Craftsman Truck Race at Lowe's Motor Speedway. Good friend Jeff Weimer helps Dan out.

© Alan Mayor Courtesy of ASCAP

2002 ASCAP #1 Party for "Beautiful Mess." *Left to right* (back): Dan, Dana, Sonny LeMaire (writer), Mike Clute (producer), Shane Minor (writer). *Left to right* (front): Jimmy, Marty, Brian, Clay Mills (writer), Connie Bradley (ASCAP)

Pictured with long-time friends and coworkers during their annual Fan Club party at a Nashville-area bowling alley. *L to r*: Dan, Gene, Marty, Brian, Scarlet Morgan (Fan Club President, also Dana's sister), Tony Morgan (Production Manager), Jimmy, Dana. "Scarlet and Tony—the best!" —Jimmy

Renée Behrman-Greiman Courtesy of Modern Management

Singing the National Anthem at the Cleveland Indians game.

ACKNOWLEDGMENTS

Thank you to the people on Music Row who helped transform our lives: Ted Greene, Renée Behrman-Greiman, Tim DuBois, Mike Clute, Monty Powell, Mike Dungan, Allen Butler, Ted Hacker, Anita Hogin, Keith Miller, Joe Bennie, Butch Waugh, Joe Galante, Renee Bell, Cindy Mabe, Jim Mazza, Ken Kragan, Al Cooley, Thomas Cain, Steve Day, Kevin Lamb, Tim Wipperman, Dale Bobo, Wally Saukerson, and Steve Thurman.

A special thanks to Tom Roland, our book writer. How you managed to navigate six life stories, six diverse backgrounds, and twenty-plus years of memories into *one* book we'll never know, but are so appreciative that you decided to join us on this journey. Janene MacIvor for your diligence and patience during this book project. We could not have pulled all the pieces together without you! Jackie Stammen for helping to tell our story through pictures. Esther Fedorkevich for sharing our story with Thomas Nelson. And to Scott McKain, our long-time friend and supporter, thank you for lending your voice to our story.

—DIAMOND RIO

Every thought . . . every action, can (and often does) affect our lives and the lives we touch. Vern and Olive Johnson never got to know the lives they would touch through their son by raising him in a house of "home made" music and leaving those instruments where he could get his hands on them. My brothers, Dick and Fred, and my sister, Hazel, have had the opportunity to see where that bit of instruction ("That's a *G* chord.") or encouragement ("That sounded pretty good, can you do it again?") has led me. So I thank *God* and my family for the gift of music.

I thank June for her unwavering, steadfast love—even through the "good ol' days" when times were bad—and for giving me two perfect daughters who are beautiful, strong, and hard working. I thank Callie Jo and Mattie Sam for loving this fool musician father who was too often gone when he was needed and for giving me two beautiful grandsons, Benjamin and Nicholas.

No one could ask for more.

I have always been greatly blessed in my life. So many opportunities, so many successes and so many incredible moments. I would like to thank and honor those who have been such an integral part of those blessings. My parents, Delmont and Karol, who gave me my faith in God, my passion for life, and my love of music; Wendee, Ben, Chad, Casey, and McKenzie for all the wonderful years; my siblings and close confidants Rhonda, Gina, and Boyd; and a special thanks to Joan Yorgason, Yolanda, Hunter, and Tanner.

It is no secret that I have been blessed beyond my wildest dreams. God continues to reach out for me in love through the people he has put in my path. At first I didn't recognize this but he started with my parents, Bill and Margie Olander, and my brother, Doug—always my supporters and my foundation. To be followed by the Rio Boys, Mike Clute, Ted Greene, and Renée Behrman-Greiman. To count these people as friends and family makes me a wealthy man.

And then add to this the center of my joy—my wife, Claudia, and boys, Maximum and Tank. Lord, I'm starting to get it . . . I've been blessed . . . I love you all.

It would take an entire chapter to acknowledge everyone. Of course, I have to recognize my mother, Leah. She instilled in me a sense of purpose and to trust in God to lead me in this life. If there are angels among us, she is one of them. A simple "thank you" to my brother, Del, could never come close to what his influence and love have done for me. He made me realize the power of dreams in a young man's life. I love you bro! My older sister Flora is possibly the most amazing woman I've ever known. She remains one of my best friends and confidants in this world. Flora, I love you more than you will ever know. Sharing my youth with my younger sister Lori had a profound impact on me. I love and pray for you, Lori, on a daily basis.

My father, Charles, never got to witness all the blessings that have come my way as a member of Diamond Rio. Dad, I never walked a mile in your shoes, and I know you did the best you could for all of us. But I want you to know that I am proud to be your son. I love you, Dad, which is something I should have said more often when I had the chance. I do not have the words to fully express the gratitude I have to God for my children Lily, Sophie, and Bentley. I'm certain that I didn't know what love was until you were born. It is now my life's purpose to always be your daddy.

To all of the great musicians and singers I've worked with over the years, thanks for how you impacted my life and career. The same thanks goes to all my friends, new and old, as well as to the women I have shared a portion of my life with. I am indeed a very blessed man.

Brian

First and foremost I would like to thank God for the gift of music. It has brought me so much joy. Next, I would like to say thanks to my bandmates for sticking by me through thick and thin. You are so talented and it has been a great pleasure to stand alongside you as you demonstrate your gifts. To my wife, Robin, I could never repay all the time, work, and encouragement you have put into my career. Your love has been a constant and you have been the hands and ears of God for me on many occasions. My girls, Isabella and Sarah, you are the light of my life and it always excites me to watch you as you are growing into godly women.

To my parents, Zane and Bertie, you have always been the example I look to for how to handle all of life's twists and turns. Thank you for introducing me to Jesus. To Scott, my brother and my biggest fan, you have been a great father to Clayton and Dylan and a great example to them and me. Love you.

Finally, I want to thank Tom Roland for all the hard work and many conversations he had to listen to while working with us on this book. I hope you got as much pleasure out of this story as we got telling it to you.

First and foremost I want to thank my Lord and Savior, Jesus Christ, for my talents and abilities to do what I do, for in him I live my life. I must thank my parents, Louise and Maurice, for raising me in a house of love and understanding and for teaching me by example the true meaning of family. My sister, Scarlet, for being there for me no matter what the reason. I will love you always. My brother-in-law, Tony, who has been the closest thing to a real brother I could ever have.

When my son Jacob was born I found out what real love is. He is a true miracle given to me, and I will cherish him forever. It's all I can do not to bust with pride every time I look at him. I love you, son! Chris and Cara, thank you for accepting me and Jacob as you have. I look forward to being a part of your lives and being there for you any way I can. My beautiful wife, Deanna. You are such an inspiration to me and a true partner in life. You have my heart, sweetie!

There are so many in my Rio life who should never be forgotten: Monty Powell, Mike Clute, Tim Dubois, Ted Hacker, Anita Hogan, Ted Greene, Renée Behrman-Grieman. This career would not have been without you. Thank you! And finally, My Rio boys, who have stood beside me for twenty years. I can't imagine making music any other way. I love ya guys!

ABOUT THE WRITER

Tom Roland is a Nashville-based entertainment journalist and author of *The Billboard Book of #1 Country Hits*. He has written about music for *The Tennessean*, *The Hollywood Reporter*, *The Orange County Register*, GACtv.com, CMT.com, *Country Weekly*, *The All-Music Guide*, *The Encyclopedia of Country Music*, and the Westwood Radio Network, among others. He is also the founder of RolandNote.com, the Ultimate Country Music Database.

Join Diamond Rio

in supporting

Big Brothers Big Sisters

 Big Brothers Big Sisters

(615)329-9191   mentorakid.org

To volunteer at your local agency, contact
BigBrothersBigSisters.org

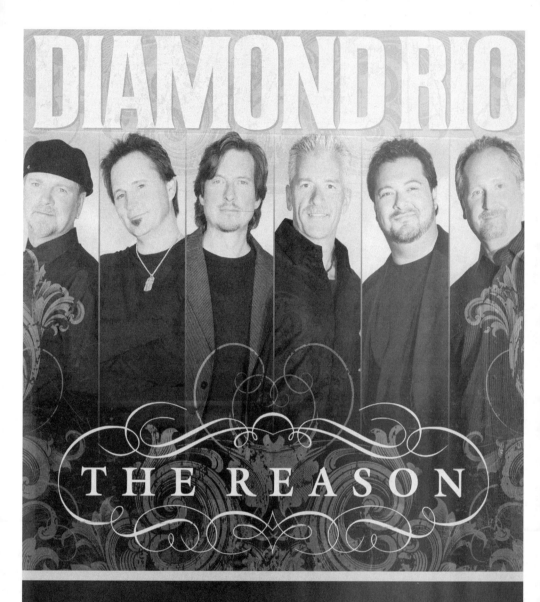

DIAMOND RIO

THE REASON